LOCAL RESOURCES FOR RURAL DEVELOPMENT

Published by New Age International (P) Ltd., Publishers
First Edition: 2013

BRANCHES

- **Bangalore** 37/10, 8th Cross (Near Hanuman Temple), Azad Nagar, Chamarajpet Bangalore-560 018, Tel.: (080) 26756823, Telefax: 26756820 **E-mail: bangalore@newagepublishers.com**
- **Chennai** 26, Damodaran Street, T. Nagar, Chennai-600 017, Tel.: (044) 24353401 Telefax: 24351463, **E-mail: chennai@newagepublishers.com**
- **Cochin** CC-39/1016, Carrier Station Road, Ernakulam South, Cochin-682 016 Tel.: (0484) 2377004, Telefax: 4051303 **E-mail: cochin@newagepublishers.com**
- **Guwahati** Hemsen Complex, Mohd. Shah Road, Paltan Bazar, Near Starline Hotel Guwahati-781 008, Tel.: (0361) 2513881, Telefax: 2543669 **E-mail: guwahati@newagepublishers.com**
- **Hyderabad** 105, 1st Floor, Madhiray Kaveri Tower, 3-2-19, Azam Jahi Road Nimboliadda, Hyderabad-500 027, Tel.: (040) 24652456 Telefax: 24652457, **E-mail: hyderabad@newagepublishers.com**
- **Kolkata** RDB Chambers (Formerly Lotus Cinema) 106A, 1st Floor S.N. Banerjee Road, Kolkata-700 014, Tel.: (033) 22273773 Telefax: 22275247, **E-mail: kolkata@newagepublishers.com**
- **Lucknow** 16-A, Jopling Road, Lucknow-226 001, Tel.: (0522) 2209578, 4045297 Telefax: 2204098, **E-mail: lucknow@newagepublishers.com**
- **Mumbai** 142C, Victor House, Ground Floor, N.M. Joshi Marg, Lower Parel Mumbai-400 013, Tel.: (022) 24927869, Telefax: 24915415 **E-mail: mumbai@newagepublishers.com**
- **New Delhi** 22, Golden House, Daryaganj, New Delhi-110 002 Tel.: (011) 23262368, 23262370, Telefax: 43551305 **E-mail: sales@newagepublishers.com**

ISBN: 978-81-224-3534-4

₹ 100.00

C-13-01-6728

Printed in India at Ajit Printers, New Delhi.

Typeset at Goswami Associates, Delhi.

PUBLISHING FOR ONE WORLD
NEW AGE INTERNATIONAL (P) LIMITED, PUBLISHERS
7/30 A, Daryaganj, New Delhi - 110002
Visit us at **www.newagepublishers.com**

LOCAL RESOURCES FOR RURAL DEVELOPMENT

R K Singal
Ph.D.
Mechanical Engineering
Educationalist and Technologist

Publishing Globally

NEW AGE INTERNATIONAL (P) LIMITED, PUBLISHERS
New Delhi • Bangalore • Chennai • Cochin • Guwahati
Hyderabad • Kolkata • Lucknow • Mumbai
Visit us at **www.newagepublishers.com**

Dedicated to the Farmer

Farmer is the founder of institution of agriculture.
He produces food and fodder for every creature.

Has set up mark on path of human evolution.
With hardwork, he has brought green revolution.

He faces all miseries and odds with determination,
And creates food buffer and wealth for the nation.

Has no hankering for riches, awards or recognition.
Believes in hardwork, simple life, that's his mission,

No grudge against those who left him in lurch,
Migrated to towns and cities for the new search.

During floods or famines, ever he is steadfast,
Ensures your feed, for self nothing may last.

Appreciate all his sacrifices and feel his pain,
When processing and eating food, waste no grain*.

*Lord Krishna to Dropadi

Preface

Geographical conditions dictate the exploitation of locally available energy sources for providing maximum amenities for the rural community. Integrated rural services can be designed from local resources available, *e.g.*, a hydro village in a hilly area, a solar village in South India or a biomass village in the plains of North India and hybrid village elsewhere. The book can be used by the village planners as guidelines. Scientists and academicians can benefit from the proposals made for taking up research and technology development projects.

The provision of domestic amenities in the villages and other rural services for community life, irrigation, agriculture and cottage industries require abundant energy. Local energy resources available in the villages and appropriate technologies developed have been explored. Alternative modes of supply of rural services and amenities using an integrated approach have been recommended. The information of the above study can be used by modern village planners.

The present book is a compilation of research papers, case studies and development projects by the author. The author is grateful to the publisher for bringing out this book in a very short time. Constructive criticism of the book is invited.

Author

Contents

Introduction

India is essentially an agricultural country with 78 per cent of its population living in rural countryside and 70 percent of its gross domestic product emanating from rural agricultural sector. There are more than 5 lakh villages scattered all over the country. About 95 percent of these villages are small villages with population less than 2000. On the average, the villages consume 150 kWh of energy per day for energising irrigation pumps for lighting, for cooking, etc. As the demand factor is very low and because these villages are widely dispersed, it is most uneconomical to electrify them from power grids. Transportation of commercial fuels like coal, diesel and petrol over long distances is very difficult and transmission and distribution of electricity through power grids to far flung areas are prohibitibly expensive. The farmers and craftsmen are not in a position to pay for high costs of energy; thus small scale industries in rural areas are reduced and there are limited irrigation possibilities in agriculture. There is a continuous flux of population to new economic centres which has created the problem of mush-rooming of slums and destruction of social life. These problems can explode with very serious consequences. The population migration must be checked by creating opportunities in rural areas. The development, welfare and prosperity of rural villages depend upon the availability of cheap and abundant energy for domestic cooking, heating and lighting, community development, irrigation water, mechanised agriculture and small industrial parks based on local resources. Solar energy and other locally available energy sources like water, current energy, biomass, wind, etc., must be utilized to boost agricultural production and agro-industries which is vitally important to raise the standard of living of growing population.

If the energy and power needs of the villages can be met from local sources, the central/zonal power grids connecting coal based thermal power plants, nuclear and hydro-plants can work in more efficient and reliable manner at high load factors feeding power only to industrial belts and big commercial centres. Tremendous investments and high power losses in long and unwieldy power lines to remote and scattered villages can be avoided.

India is bestowed with plentiful of sunshine for 250–300 days per year. In South and Central India, the annual average daily incidence of solar energy is about 4.5 kWh/m^2 with the maximum exceeding even 7.0 kWh/m^2. Therefore, solar energy offers an attractive solution to rural energy problems in India where power requirements are small and in remote areas where application of solar energy is most suited. There is an urgent need to the use/development of following solar gadgets for rural villages:

- solar cookers which must fit well with the age-old habits of conventional cooking and should be accepted by the rural population in India without any reservations;
- small solar driven refrigerators for the preservation of food, storage of milk and other products to improve rural income;
- solar water irrigation pumps to boost agricultural production and provide drinking water which is vitally important in view of growing population;
- solar water heaters and dryers for agricultural products;
- small power plants to produce electricity for domestic and street lighting and cottage industries.

Rural India is very diverse in topography, climate and natural resource availability. When coastal areas are plentiful in wind energy and tidal and wave power in the oceans, the alpine areas are abundant in water current energy in streams and forest residues as biomass. Deserts are bestowed with high solar insolations, plain fields have excess of agricultural residues for production of power and again water current energy of rivers and irrigation canals can be exploited to install small micro hydro power plants. Therefore, solar energy should be integrated with other energy sources locally availablc for meeting the total energy and power requirements. Depending upon the location, the other resources of the village which can be exploited to design and build hybrid energy systems are:

- water current energy in the rivers, streams and irrigation canals where microhydro power plants can be installed for generation of electric power;
- biomass for generation of power by direct burning in fluidised bed combustors for generation of steam for a turbogenerator or production of fuel gas by gasification for running an I.C. Engine plant;
- animal wastes for generation of biogas for running an I.C. Engine or cooking gas or street lighting;
- wind energy for water pumping;
- tidal and wave energy for power generation.

The author has been engaged in the investigation, planning, design and development of rural energy systems based on non-conventional energy sources and results of his findings and experiences are given in the following chapters.

PART 1
RURAL TECHNOLOGIES

Chapter 1

Rural Services

1.1 SYNOPSIS

The provision of domestic amenities in the villages and other rural services for community life, irrigation, agriculture and cottage industries require abundant energy. Local energy resources available in the villages and appropriate technologies developed have been explored. Alternative modes of supply of rural services and amenities using an integrated approach have been recommended. The information of the above study can be used by modern village planners.

1.2 INTRODUCTION

In most of the rural communities, quality of life is extremely low. There are people having no asset to talk about, no land, no shelter, no food; and are forced to live a miserable life under the trees because of their financial distress. Even when there is enough food, sanitation, medical care, education, lighting, hot water and community life are severely lacking.

A minimum shelter or dwelling is a must for any human being next to food to enable him to live a useful social life. The desire to build a reasonably good house of one's own with maximum possible amenities is cherished by one and all.

In order to improve the living standards of rural population, a number of projects like 'Low Cost Housing' or 'Houses for the Millions' have been launched by Central and State Governments to build new and low cost houses. The provision of maximum possible amenities with these houses and other rural services require cheap and abundant energy for domestic cooking, food production and processing, heating and lighting, community development, irrigation water, mechanised agriculture and cottage industries, based on local resources. Transportation of electricity through grids to far flung areas are prohibitively expensive. Supplying commercial fuels like coal, diesel and petrol over long distances is very difficult.

An attempt has been made in this chapter to identify need for domestic amenities and other rural services and their present status of supply. Potential of renewable alternative energy sources locally available in the villages and status of supplementary and appropriate technologies developed have been surveyed in details. Alternative modes of supply of these services based on local resources and available technologies have been explored. Under the severe constraints of resources and paucity of funds, an integrated approach to supply of rural services is recommended.

1.3 RURAL SERVICES

Domestic amenities for a typical village have been identified in Table 1.1. Cooking energy is the main requirement followed by drinking water, wash water, lighting and heating. The common modes of energy inputs presently used are listed in the 2nd column of the Table. The proposed alternative sources are shown in the 3rd column. The potential of these resources and latest technology status are discussed in the following paragraphs. Typical services for community life are included in Table 1.2. The community services as on today are absent. Therefore, alternative sources are recommended in the Table. Similarly, the utilities in the form of electricity, water and steam are needed for the development of cottage industries in the villages. The potential technologies based on renewable and local energy sources are listed in Table 1.3.

Table. 1.1 Domestic Amenities

Sr. No.	*Amenities*	*Common Mode of Energy Input (Present)*	*Potential Alternate Sources (Proposed)*
1.	Cooking	Wood, Cowdung	Biogas, solar cooking plates.
2.	Drinking water	Animal power, Human labour	Wind, water current energy of water, electricity, solar pump.
3.	Wash water	Open surface water	Water pumps run from wind, solar, micro hydro, electricity
4.	Lighting	Kerosene	Biogas lanterns, solar lights, electricity.
5.	Heating	Wood, cowdung	Solar, biogas heaters.

Table 1.2 Community Services

Sr. No.	*Services*	*Common Mode of Energy Input (Present)*	*Potential Alternate Sources (Proposed)*
1.	Radio, TV sets	Nil	Solar, Electricity
2.	Street lighting	Nil	Solar, biogas electricity
3.	Milk chilling	Nil	Solar refrigeration, electricity

Table 1.3 Utilities for Industries

Sr. No.	*Utilities*	*Common Mode of Energy Input (Present)*	*Potential Alternate Sources (Proposed)*
1.	Electricity	Nil	Micro Hydro. Solar, wind, biogas generators.
2.	Water	Open ponds, canal system	Wind, Solar, Micro Hydro, Biogas water pumps.
3.	Hot water/steam	Wood, Cowdung	Solar heaters/boilers on biogas, biomass.

The main human efforts in rural areas are directed towards securing sufficient food. Nearly 65–80 percent of energy consumed is in the food chain systems. The typical food supply systems and traditional energy inputs are illustrated in Figs. 1.1, 1.2 and 1.3. Potential areas of substitution by solar energy are also marked in the same figures. It is important to note the proposal for redivision of activities between rural and urban regions as marked in the figures 1.2 and 1.3 so that more value added activities are shifted to villages for rural prosperity. (on next page)

1.4 ALTERNATIVE ENERGY SOURCES

India is bestowed with plenty of sunshine for 250–300 days per year. In South and Central India, the annual average daily incidence of solar energy is about 4.5 kWh/m^2. with the maximum even exceeding 7 kWh/m^2. Therefore, solar energy can be used to solve some of the energy problems in rural India. Solar energy can be integrated with locally available energy sources. Depending upon the location, the other sources of the village which can be exploited are:

(*i*) water current energy in the rivers and irrigation canals where micro hydro plants working on low/zero head turbines can be installed for generation of electricity and direct pumping of water. It is estimated that 5000 MW capacity of power can be created in India with the help of small hydro turbines of 200 kW to 1000 kW capacity each.

(*ii*) biomass for generation of power by direct burning in fluidised-bed combustors for generation of steam for a thermal power plant or production of fuel gas by gasification and running I.C. Engine plant. The estimated production of agricultural residues in India is 200 million tonnes per year and that of wood is 130 million tonnes. At an energy conversion rate of 35 percent total useful potential is about 75000 MW. The fluidised bed units can be used in conjunction with various configurations of power cycles using steam turbines, gas turbines, combined cycles with and without cogeneration.

(*iii*) animal wastes for generation of biogas for running an I.C. Engine or cooking gas. The biogas consumption is about 0.46 m^3 per kWh which can be obtained from 13.5 kg of cattle dung. *i.e* daily product of one cattle.

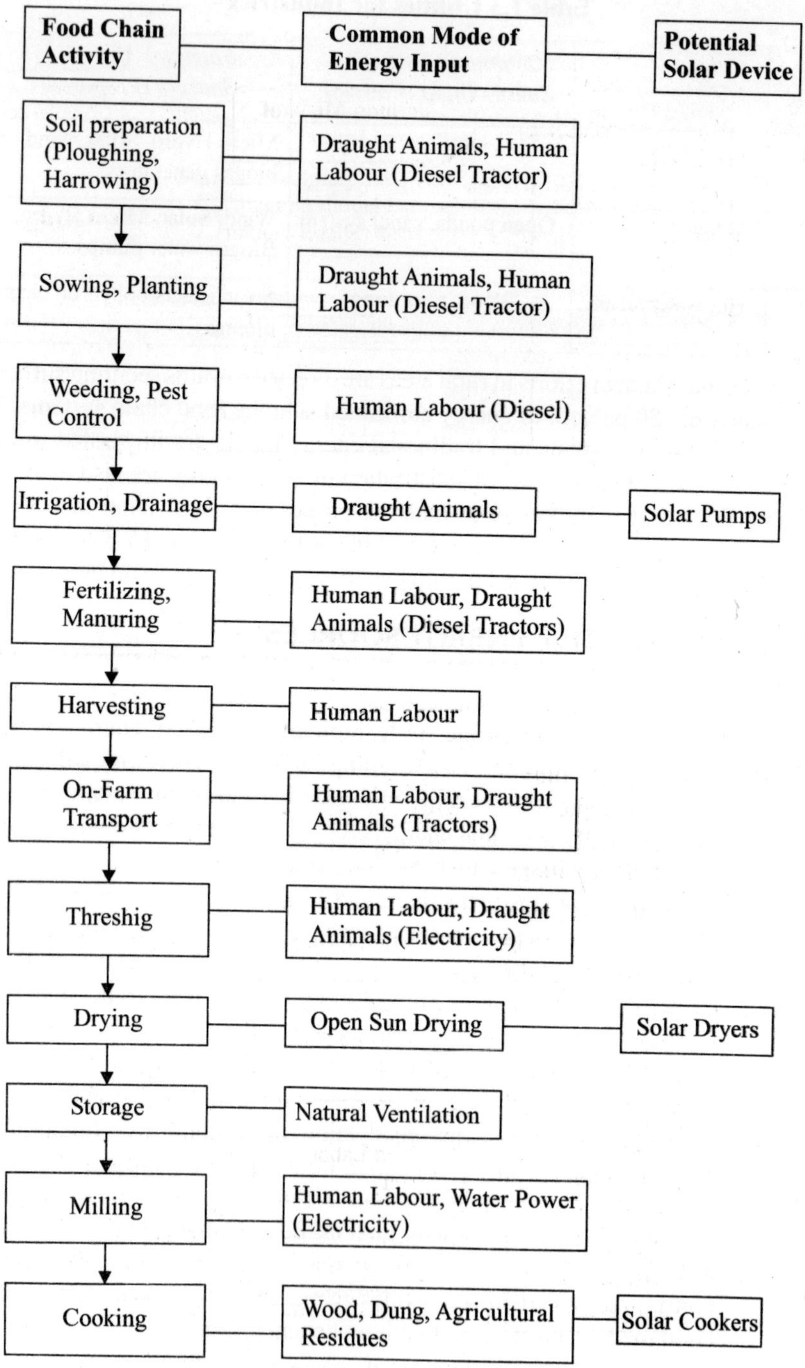

Fig. 1.1. Imperishable food supply system

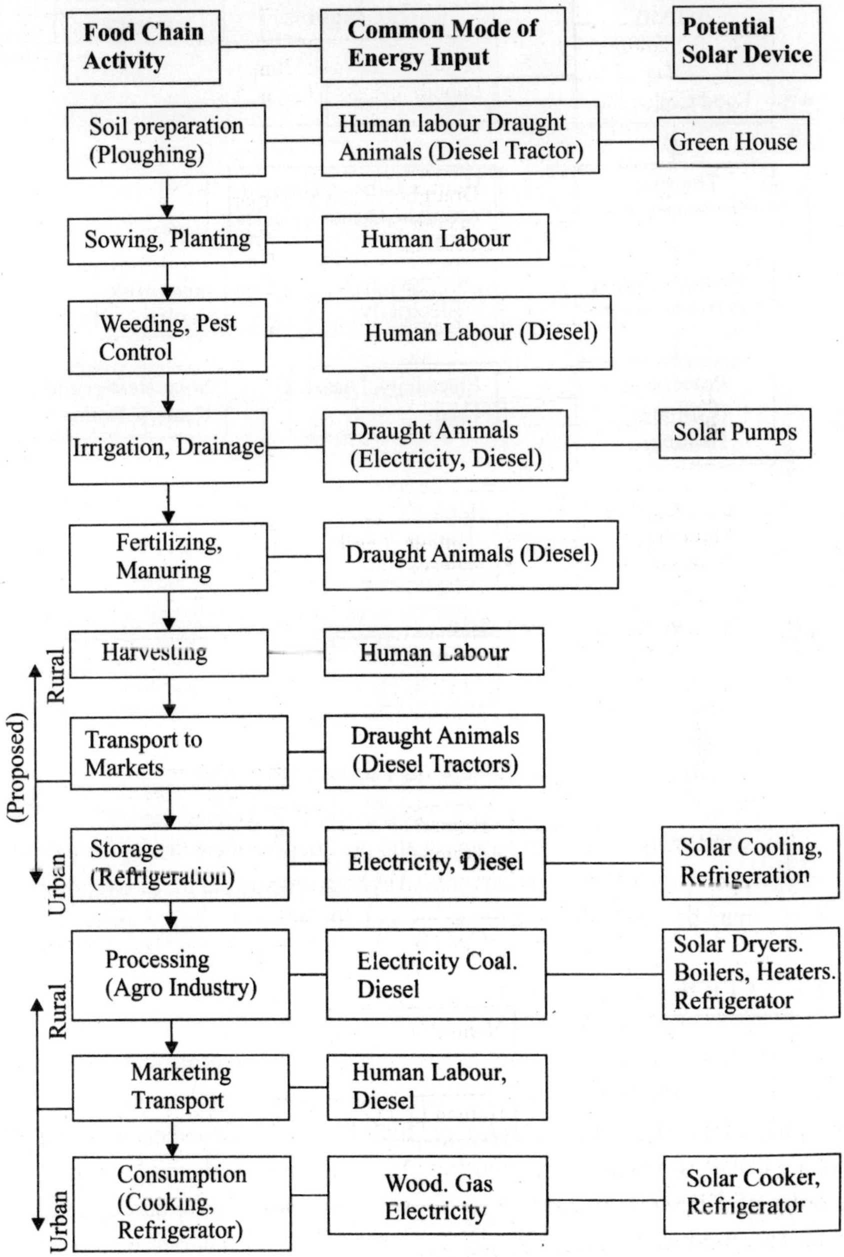

Fig. 1.2. Perishable food supply system

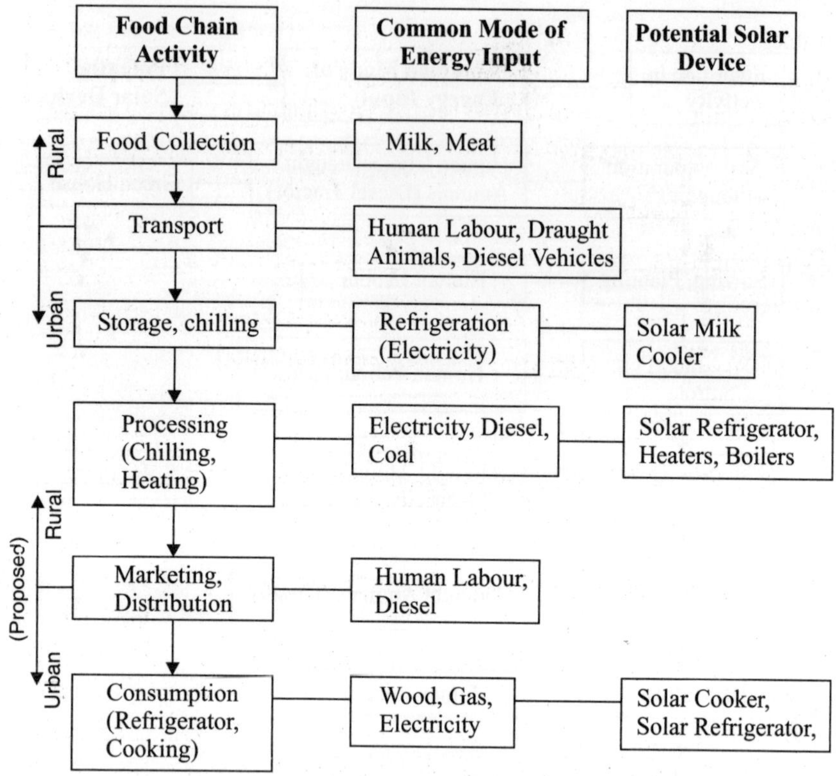

Fig. 1.3. Animal husbandary food supply system

(*iv*) wind energy for water pumping and production of electricity. Depending upon local wind conditions annual average energy per m^2 of swept surface may be 100 kWh for calm areas and 500 kWh for windy areas.

1.5 COOKING ENERGY

Eighty percent of the basic energy needs of rural India is provision of cooking energy, which amounts to 0.5 to 1 kWh/person/day with a peak of 0.2 to 1.2 kW per capita. It is mostly met from traditional fuels like firewood and cowdung cakes. Cooking usually takes place on open-fire places which have thermal efficiency of the order of 5 percent. In case where firewood is scarce, dung and agricultural residues are used. If too much dung and residues are taken off agricultural land, the soil may become slowly depleted of essential nutrients, causing gradually decreasing yields on an increasing demand for synthetic fertilizers.

1.5.1 Hot Plate Type Solar Cooker

The Government of India is trying to introduce box-type solar cookers with financial subsidies but with poor success due to many technical drawbacks in the design. The temperature obtained is less than 100°C and is insufficient for chapati making and frying which are very important cooking processes. There is no provision for storage of heat and cooking has to be carried out while the sun is shinning which is an odd time for preparing dinner and breakfast. Cooking has to be carried out in the open without privacy and in the sun which is very inconvenient to the housewife. In order to overcome all these difficulties, a small family size solar cooker was designed and fabricated at REC, Kurukshetra. It consists of a flat plate with mirror boosters, an oil storage tank, a thermosyphon system, a heat pipe and a control valve. It would just replace a bottled gas cooking range. There are no operating and maintenance expenses.

1.5.2 Biogas Plate

The technology for conversion of animal wastes into biogas via anaerobic digestion is well established and quite a large number of biogas plants both community type and individual type are already in operation. The biogas obtained from 13.5 kg of cattle dung. *i.e.* daily produce of one cattle, is sufficient to meet the cooking energy requirements of two persons and surprisingly, the ratio of human beings to cattle in an Indian village is two. The gas produced can be easily transported to specially designed gas plates through network of HDPE pipes.

1.6 WATER SYSTEM

Drip irrigation of corn, wheat, cotton, millets requires 25 m^3 of water per hectare-day; whereas flood irrigation of rice, sugarcane. etc., would require 50 to 60 m^3 of water per hectare, day. In addition, water requirements for live stock is 40 to 50 litres per head-day. The lifting height of water varies from a few meters to 30 m. The equivalent anergy requirements would be 135 W per hectare for surface water and 400 W per hectare for ground water.

Out of the total 143 million hectares of land under cultivation in the country, hardly 43 million hectares (a barely 25 percent of the land under cultivation) is irrigated. Out of this irrigated area, 23 million hectares are served by tube-wells, ponds or such similar minor irrigation schemes. There are about 2 to 3 million open wells in our country which are motorised. Various modes of irrigation and water supply schemes based on non-conventional energy sources have been developed.

1.6.1 Solar Water Pumps

The National Physical Laboratory, New Delhi has developed Abhimanyu Solar Pump of 1 kW rating using R114. The total cost of the components (condenser, boiler, expansion motor, storage tank, collector assembly and pump) and development charges is of the order of ₹ 37,000.

1.6.2 Solar Photovoltaic Water Pumping System

The Central Electronics Ltd. Sahibabad (UP) has developed a photovoltaic system at a cost of ₹ 40,000 which can give an average water output of 30 to 40 m^3 per day with a maximum total head of 10 m. It is highly subsidised and installed at a cost of only ₹ 5,000.

1.7 WIND MILL

The specifications of a propeller type wind mill-pump set has been standardised for installation in India are:

Tower Height	:	7 m.
No. of Propellers	:	12
Rotor Diameters	:	5 m
Machine Power Ratio	:	0.36
Water Depth	:	20 m
Maximum daily output	:	23 m^3 at a wind speed of 10 m/s.

Total cost of machine including transportation and erection is ₹ 11,750 and a similar expenditure is to be incurred on well boring and construction of storage tank. The Government of India provides a subsidy of ₹ 7,500.

1.8 BIOGAS ENGINES

The biogas engines for pumpsets produced in India are essentially diesel engines where air intake is connected to biogas supply. The diesel is required for starting the engine and 20 percent diesel and 80 percent biogas are mixed automatically to produce power. The biogas consumption is about 0.46 m^3/kWh which can be obtained from 13.5 kg of cattle dung. The price of a typical 3.7 kW, 1500 rpm biogas engine with centrifugal pump of 100 × 100 mm including accessories and trolley is about ₹ 6,500. It is subsidised by Government agencies. The cost of a typical gobar gas plant of 85 m^3 capacity is about one lac rupees.

1.8.1 Biomass Gasifiers

The agricultural and forest residues can be first dried in solar driers to restrict the moisture content below 15 percent. These are pressed in compaction briquetting machines to prepare feed size of 50 to 75 mm for the gasifier. On an average 1 kg of biosmass produces 2.5 nm^3 of fuel gas and 1 kWh of shaft energy to drive irrigation pump. The total cost of a biomass gasifier with gas cooler and scrubber of 15 m^3/hr capacity, 5 kW/1500 rpm diesel engine and 100 × 100 mm centrifugal pump with accessories and controls is about ₹ 37,000.

1.8.2 Water Mills

Poncet water wheel or a Darrieus turbine rotor can be submerged in a river, water stream or canal to tap current energy from water speed as low as 1 m/s. The mechanical energy thus obtained is used for driving irrigation pumps. Such floating water mills can be used in conjunction with Himalayan Mills and Hydraulic rams to meet the total energy requirements of a village in mountaneous region for irrigation and drinking water and all the electrical power for domestic, community and industrial purposes.

1.9 OTHER SOLAR GADGETS

Photovoltaic solar systems for street lighting, solar TV sets, solar driers for agricultural products, solar kiln, distillation plants, air and water heaters have been developed and are used to provide rural amenities.

1.9.1 Solar Refrigerator

At the 1975 UNESCO Conference on Solar Energy, several developing countries stated that small solar driven units are urgently needed for preservation of food in rural areas where little electric power is available. A study and design project was undertaken, at REC, Kurukshetra for the development of a small solar refrigerator, Solid absorption zeolite refrigeration cycle was adopted because of absence of moving parts, toxic and corrosive chemicals and expectation of long and trouble-free operation. It was designed for fitting onto the cabinet of the present 165 1 capacity domestic refrigerator. It consists of a 1.5 m^2 flat plate collector filled with 50 mm thick zeolite and can produce 9 kg of ice in 8 hours. The project experience can be used for the development of small solar cold storages for preservation of food in rural areas.

1.9.2 Solar Milk Cooler

Nearly 500/600 litres of milk per village is sold as liquid milk per day and its chilling is done by the agencies procuring it. A village level chilling/cooling facility will make possible the collection once in a day resulting in large savings. For example, reduction in route kilometerage alone can result in savings of about 12.5 percent of procurement price. Rural processing of milk will also add value to the produce and increase rural income. The zeolite solar refrigerator can be attached to cooling-cum-storage tank. The water refrigerant circulates by thermosyphon effect in the tank walls and acts as a very efficient heat exchanger, reducing the temperature difference between milk and water vapour to less than 0.5°C.

1.10 CONCLUSIONS

Geographical conditions dictate the exploitation of locally available energy sources for providing maximum amenities for the rural community. Integrated rural services can be designed from local resources available, for example a hydro village in a hilly area, a solar village in south India or a biomass village in the plains of north India and hybrid village elsewhere. The study material of this paper can be used by the village planners as guidelines. The scientists and academicians can benefit from the proposals made for taking up research and technology development projects.

Chapter 2

An Energy Sufficient Village

2.1 ABSTRACT

Cow has been used as a unit around which sound economy of a village had been built and sustained in ancient India. This chapter proposes to remodel the system and cow has been evaluated as a unique energy conversion unit for an energy sufficient village. It has been proved with the help of suitable data that with certain new technological inputs, the old model can be used to meet all the energy requirements of a village.

2.2 BACKGROUND

Lord Krishna had been a colourful and many facet personality. With rural brought-up, he showed himself as possessor of great physical prowess and went on, later in life, to demonstrate that he could win great battle by shear planning and diplomacy without active involvement otherwise. As a preacher of Bhagwat Gita, his practical philosophy of Karma Yoga has overshadowed his many other original and unconventional trends in thinking. One of his great contributions to suffer was in the field of rural economy. He visualised cow as an economic unit around which sound economy of a village could be built and sustained. More interesting was his commitment to this idea and aggressiveness he used for the implementation of his programme.

2.3 INTRODUCTION

The post independence uneven development and industrialisation has created moral, mental and spiritual degradation and frustration among rural population in India, who have remained isolated from the economic planning and growth. It has now become compelling to think about the 80 percent of rural population for the satisfaction of their basic needs, their self-reliance based on social participation and harmony with the environment to ensure the sustainability of their development.

The solution of the problem lies in making available cheap and abundant supply of energy for cooking, heating, lighting, community development, pumping of water for drinking and irrigation, powered agriculture and small scale industries. The energy conversion techniques should be pollution free, based on renewable and locally available sources and appropriate technology involving local manpower, local materials and local resources which can be locally managed and amalgamated with the rural surroundings.

In this context, the wisdom of Lord Krishna can be tested. His idea of cow as a unit for rural economy can be remodelled to evaluate it as energy conversion unit. The cow eats biomass (fodder) and gives out milk and cowdung which can be properly processed to yield useful energy. Cow is symbollic and includes buffalo and other milching and associated animals.

2.4 RESOURCES FROM A COW

Cow is a very revered animal in Hinduism because of plentiness of resources obtained from her. The daily income resources are milk and cow-dung. Milk is one of the most wonderful and almost complete food available in nature. Not only it has high nutrient constituents but also it is used for a large variety of domestic and industrial food products in the form of curds and kafeers, butter and butterghee, cream, cheese, sweets, milk-powder, ice-creams, etc., etc. There are people who live on cow milk only and can meet their full energy (food) requirements from it.

Cowdung is another wonderful waste to meet the fuel and fertilizer requirements in rural areas. A major portion of collected cowdung is used as a domestic fuel after drying the cowdung cakes. The above together with some supplements of agrowastes and firewood meet the fuel requirements of the rural population in India.

The cow periodically gives birth to draught animals which contribute substantially to the energy demands of agriculture, irrigation and transport sectors.

Useful food and industrial raw materials are obtained after the death of cow, *i.e*, meat, leather, glues, blood, bones, etc. Therefore, cow is very useful as a source of raw materials for Dairy and Milkfood industries, Meat industry, Leather, Chemicals and Glue industries, etc.

2.4.1 Milk and Milk Products

The milk yield of cow and buffaloes varies widely from 5 litres to 30 litres per day; the total milk production in India may be of the order of 700 million litres per day. The daily calories need of man varies from 2500 (light work) to 5000 (heavy work). Although, man does not depend wholly on milk and milk products for his calories intake, however, a model can be conceived to evaluate the contribution of cow to meet the total energy intake of men.

The calories content of some milk product are: cow milk (670 calories per litre), buffalo milk (950 calories per litre), curd (600 calories per litre), cheese (3480 calories per kg), butter (7290 calories per kg) and butter ghee (8280 calories per kg). It may, therefore, be assumed that cattle milk can give on an average 900 calories per litre of milk. Thus the present cattle population in India can fully meet the total energy requirements of 180 million people of average size.

The energy equivalents of man are: 1050 kJ per manhour; 840 kJ per woman hour and 500 kJ per childhour. Therefore, the total energy equivalent of milk production in India is 4,16,000 MWh .

2.4.2 Draught Animals

Draught animal is an excellent energy device readily available in the rural scene and within the means and technical competence of the farmer for ploughing and water lifting and small scale cart operators for transportation (1). In India, there may be about 130 million draught animals including young stock; and 80 million work animals ploughing two-thirds of land and carry two-thirds of rural transportation. These are more economical than tractors for ploughing farms of sizes less than four hectares and more competent than trucks for handling vehicles for small scale transportation (about one tonne) over short distances (below 20 km). Trucks become economical only for heavier loads of 3–5 tonnes and when distances moved per day are more than 200 km.

The animal power is 9650 kJ/Bullock-hour and total draught animal energy of working animals in India is 215,000 MWh. Five pairs of bullocks can replace one tractor and therefore, eight million tractors can be replaced by 80 million work animals, saving huge amount of capital investment in addition to avoidance of dependence on scarce diesel/kerosene oil, mostly imported by India. On an average a buffalo gives 6 to 7 births and a cow 10 to 12 births per life. Therefore, the cow contributes substantially to this unique form of renewable energy source.

2.4.3 Cow Dung

The cattle population in India is 235 million heads with a dry dung yield of about 170 million tonnes per year. The composted manure prepared from cow dung has 0.75 to 1 percent Nitrogen after losses and is used as a fertilizer for agriculture. The collection efficiency of cowdung is 70 percent and loss constituent of 30 percent pollutes the environment.

The prevalent practice of burning cowdung cakes, firewood and farm wastes in rural India is not an attractive one. A major portion of the collected cowdung is used as domestic fuel after drying the cowdung cakes. The practice of making cowdung cakes is unhygenic and low combustion efficiency of 11 percent is wasteful. This can rapidly result in the problem of deforestation on one hand and loss of soil nutrients on the other.

2.4.3.1 Biogas

The livestock and even human wastes have much potential as an energy source in developing countries via anaerobic digestion; the wastes are treated with simultaneous evolution of methane fuel and retention of nitrogen and other vital plant nutrients in the remaining sludge, which can be recycled as a fertilizer. 'Biogas' generation is a versatile process ranging from small domestic 'Gobar' gas plants catered by a few cows to much bigger community type plants where relatively large volume of cowdung is continuously available. These depend greatly on hot climate and manual labour for its functioning. These can go a long way to providing much of the energy required by a large population.

The technology for conversion of animal wastes into biogas via anaerobic digestion is well established, and quite a large number of biogas plants (about one lakhs) are already in operation in Indian villages (2). Our country has a potential of producing about 22000 million Cubic meters of biogas with a heating value of 21kJ per cubic meter.

The Gobar gas plants are mainly developed by Khadi and Village Industries Commission, New Delhi. In every state, Khadi and Village Industries Boards look after the erection work of the Gobar gas Plants. The Ministry of Agriculture, Government of India is also helping for the construction of Gobar Gas Plant.

For a typical Indian village of population 500, the number of cattle would probably be around 250. The amount of dry dung collected from them would be approximately 180 tonnes per year calculated on the basis of 13.5 kg of cattle dung as daily produce of one cattle.. This would be more than sufficient to meet the complete fuel and other energy requirements of the village population on conversion to methane.

The human wastes can also be used for production of biogas. Community latrines can be planned in the villages for collection of night soil for feeding to Biogas plants. Wastes of 200 persons can be used to produce about 5 cubic meter of gas per day to extract 12 kWh of equivalent energy.

2.4.3.2 Biogas engines

The requirement of Indian farmers for engines varies from 3.7 kW to 7.5 kW in vertical high speed and vertical low speed types all over the country. Normally, the engine runs on an average for 5 hours per day. Biogas produced by a digester that is functioning well is approximately 65 percent methane and has a heating value of nearly 21000 kJ per cubic meter. The biogas engines for pumpsets produced in India are essentially diesel engines where air intake is connected to biogas supply. The diesel is required for starting the engine and about 20 percent diesel and 80 percent biogas are mixed automatically to produce power for running the pumpset. The biogas consumption is about 0.46 cubic meter per kWh which can be obtained from 13.5 kg of cattle dung, *i.e.*, daily produce of one cattle. The price of a typical 3.7 kW, 1500 rpm biogas engine with centrifugal pump of 100 × 100 mm including accessories and trolley is about ₹ 15000. It is financed by the State Agro Industries and Land Development Banks and other nationalised banks and subsidised by Government. The cost of a typical Gobar gas plant of 85 cubic meters capacity is about ₹ 1.5 lakhs.

2.4.3.3 Spent slurry

The digestion process in the Gobar gas plant enhances the fertilizer quality of cowdung. The nitrogen content of the spent slurry from the plant is very high, 1.5 to 2 percent which is double the nitrogen content of original cowdung.

2.5 CONCLUSIONS

The cow is a very useful animal converting solar energy through biomass into useful products and services. It is an unique energy conversion unit. At the same time it should be remembered that cow lives largely on crop residues, grass and other such products which are not readily useful to man. Also they graze on marginal lands where edible crops cannot be raised.

Lord Krishna's wisdom is fully vindicated . It is proposed that rural economy should be planned with cow as energy conversion and economic unit. More important is that the commitment and aggressiveness of Lord Krishna must be used in the implementation of the plans. The cattle breeding, health care, research and development in anaerobic digestion, farm and transport implements should be taken up more vigorously.

2.6 REFERENCES

1. Ramaswamy, N.S. "*Appropriate Technology_Draught Animal Systems*", Seminar on Appropriate Rural Technology Strategies for Development and Extension, Lucknow, April 16–17,1984.

Chapter 3

Non-Conventional Energy for Lift Irrigation

3.1 INTRODUCTION

India is essentially an agricultural country with 70 percent of its population living in rural villages and 70 percent of its gross domestic product emanating from the rural agricultural sector. There are nearly 350000 villages with a population less than 500. These villages are remotely scattered and widely dispersed from the industrial belt. Their energy needs are meagre. On the average, these villages need 150 kWh of energy per day for energizing irrigation pumps, for lighting, for cooking, etc. Drip irrigation of corn, wheat, cotton, millets requires about 25 m^3 of water per hectare-day whereas flood irrigation of rice, sugarcane, etc. would require 50 to 60 m^3 of water per hectare-day. In addition, water requirement for live stock is 40 to 50 litres per head-day. The lifting height of water varies from a few meters to 30 m. The equivalent energy requirement would be 135 W per hectare for surface water and 400 W per hectare for ground water.

As the load factor is very low and because these villages are widely dispersed, it is most uneconomical to electrify them. Only 11 percent of these villages have been electrified so far. It is equally difficult to reach them with fossil fuels. Consequently, they have to find an energy source which is locally available. If locally available energy sources could be converted to mechanical energy to drive irrigation pumps, the rural scene in India would change appreciably, and it would help to boost agricultural production which is vitally important in view of growing population.

Out of the 143 million hectares of land under cultivation in the country, hardly 43 million hectares — a barely 25 percent of the land under cultivation is irrigated. Out of this irrigated area, 23 million hectare are served by tube-wells, ponds or such similar minor irrigation schemes. There are about 2–3 millions of open wells in our country which are not yet motorized.

The non-conventional and renewable energy sources have assumed considerable importance and urgency after oil crisis. Various modes of irrigation schemes based on non-conventional energy sources have been discussed in the following paragraphs which are immediately available.

3.2 SOLAR ENERGY

India is bestowed with plentiful of sunshine for 250–300 days per year. In south and central India, the annual average daily incidence of solar energy is about 4.5 kWh/ m^2 with the maximum exceeding even 7.0 kWh/ m^2. Therefore, solar energy offers a viable solution if it can be converted to mechanical energy to drive irrigation pumps. Requirements of small-scale irrigation and domestic plants are well within the reach of solar energy pumps. A pair of bullocks working continuously can raise one m^3 of water per hour from a depth of 30 m. The equivalent of this work can be done by an electric motor pump rated at 0.8 kW for which a solar pump can be designed.

3.2.1 Solar Water Pumps

Organic vapour Ranking Cycle systems with rotary machines or screw expander or reciprocating engine or spiral expanders can be used to drive water pumps, Sofretes of France have developed simple, rugged, reliable solar water pumps which work on low temperature thermodynamic cycle. It consist of solar flat plate collectors with methyl chloride as heating fluid, a heat exchanger to transfer heat to working fluid (Butane or Freon), expansion motor working at 150/200 rpm and water pump with hydraulic transmission. A collector area of 60 m^2, for example, can lift 10 m^3/hr of water over a height of 12 m. A collector surface area of 1500 m^2 can be used to lift 150 m^3/hr of water over a height of 40 m to irrigate 20 to 30 hectare of land.

The National Physical Laboratory, New Delhi has developed Abhimanyu Solar Pump of 1 kW rating using R114. An area of 10 m^2 is used to operate the pump for four hours a day. When not pumping, it can be used to drive a generator or thresher or a lathe. The total cost of the components (condenser, boiler, expansion motor, storage tank, collector assembly and pump) is ₹ 12500 and if we include the development charges, overheads and labour for assembly, the total cost will be of the order of ₹ 37000.

3.2.2 Solar Photo Voltaic Water Pumping System

In a solar photovoltaic water pumping system, the sun light is directly converted into electricity and this energy is used to run an electric motor pumpset. The Central Electronics Ltd., Sahibabad (UP) have developed the following system:

Solar Panel	:	300 W (peak)
	:	2.4 × 2.5 m (size)
System Voltage	:	60 V DC nominal
Motor pump set	:	DC motor-centrifugal pump monoblock configuration.
Peak water output	:	1.5 to 2.0 l/s.
Average water output (at 5 m total head)	:	30 to 40 m^3 per day.

Max Suction Head : 6 m

Max total head : 10 m.

The solar array consists of 5 rows of 4 modules each. Each module consists of 36 cells each 76 mm diameter connected in series to generate about 16 peak watts of power at incident radiation of 100 mW/cm^2 at 28°C. Four such modules are connected in series and five such series connected module chains are kept in parallel. The complete array is mounted on an angle iron structure which can be oriented to face the sun. The system can be provided with storage batteries and power conditioning equipment. The total cost of the system including solar photovoltaic array, on off switch, motor pump set, accessories including suction and delivery valves and piping is about ₹ 40000 which is highly subsidised and installed at a cost of ₹ 5000 only for a small or marginal farmer.

3.3 WIND ENERGY

The wind is a free, clean, inexhaustible energy source. Until this century, it has served mankind well by sailing ships, driving windmills to grind grains and pump water and even generating small amounts of electricity. The support for wind power is increasing again due to doubtful position of fossil fuels and safety of nuclear power. Following a better understanding of the aerodynamics of rotating aerolifts, there is a revival of interest in harvesting of wind energy. For a wind speed of 10 m/s, the effective power obtained is 0.25 kW per m^2 of swept area. As wind velocity of 10 m/s occurs only for a few hours a year, the mean annual available power is very less. Depending upon local wind conditions, the annual available energy per m^2 of swept surface may vary between 100 kWh for calm areas and 500 kWh for very windy areas. At least 25 percent of our land especially coastal areas are situated in reasonably windy areas. The scope for small water pumping wind mill is quite significant.

The wind energy data for Veraval situated on the windy west coast of India is as follows:

Max usable energy in wind for 30 m^2 swept area	:	20,000 kWh
Machine Power Ratio	:	0.2
Annual power output	:	4,000 kWh
Water depth	:	10 m
Average daily output	:	273 m^3 of water
Max daily output	:	2428 m^3 of water

Windmill WP-2 developed at National Aeronautical Laboratory, Bangalore can pump 2.9 m^3/hr against a head of 10 m in wind speed of 3.5 m/s. A sail wind developed at the above laboratory uses six triangular canvas sails on a rotor of 7 m diameter and pumps 5.4 m^3/hr against a head of 10 m in wind speed of 3.5 m/s.

The specification of a propeller type wind mill pump set which has been standardised for installation in India are:

Tower Height	:	7 m
No. of Propellers	:	12
Rotor Diameter	:	5 m
Machine Power Ratio	:	0.36
Water Depth	:	20 m
Max Daily Output	:	23 m^3 at a wind speed of 10 m/s.

Total cost of machine including transportation and erection is ₹ 11750 and a similar expenditure is to be incurred on well/boring and construction of storage tank. The Government provides a subsidy of ₹ 7500.

The current philosophy is to use the same wind rotor for different wind regimes with modified downstream components and higher ratings. Given that the power contained in the wind goes as cube of the wind velocity, a two-fold increase in the wind velocity implies an eight fold increase in the power contained.

The windmills installed so far are not only of small sizes (about 5 m diameter), but these also require high maintenance support. Research efforts are now needed so as to reduce the maintenance expenditure of windmills to minimum, *i.e.*, to occasional oiling and changing the pump washer. Somewhat larger windmills are required to be developed than presently available. It is also needed to develop cheaper and simpler S-rotors which can cut in at low wind speeds of 1.5–2 m/s to cover wider areas of regions.

3.4 BIOGAS ENGINES

The technology for conversion of animal wastes into biogas via anaerobic digestion is well established, and quite a large number of biogas plants (about one lakhs) are already in operation. Our country has a potential of producing about 22,000 million cubic meters of biogas. The Gobar gas plants are mainly developed by Khadi and Village Industries Commission, New Delhi and in every state, Khadi and Village Industries Boards look after the erection work of the Gobar gas plants. The Ministry of Agriculture is also helping for the construction of Gobar gas plants.

It consists of a well made of bricks putting 2 to 3 steel rods to make it more strong and plastered. The top of the well is covered by 1.6 mm thick steel sheet floating dome. The design of the above plant is available from Khadi and Village Industries Commission. The size to the plant will depend upon the gas requirement by the engine.

The requirement of Indian farmers for engine varies from 3.7 kW to 7.5 kW in vertical high speed and vertical slow speed types all over the country. Normally, the engine runs an average for 5 hours per day. Biogas produced by a digester that is functioning well is approximately 65 percent CH_4 and has a heating value of approximately 21000 kJ/m^3. The biogas engines for pumpets produced in India are essentially diesel engines where air intake is connected to biogas supply. The diesel is required for starting the engine and about 20 percent diesel and 80 percent biogas are mixed automatically to produce power for running the pumpset. The biogas consumption is about 0.46 m^3/kWh which can be obtained from 13.5 kg of cattle dung, *i.e.,* daily product of one cattle. The price of a typical 3.7 kW, 1500 rpm biogas engine with centrifugal pump of 100 × 100 mm including accessories and trolley is about ₹ 6500. It is subsidised by the Government and can be financed by the State Agro Industries, Land Development Banks and all nationalised banks. The cost of a typical gobar gas plant of 85 m^3 capacity is about ₹ one lakh.

The human wastes can also be used for production of biogas. Community latrines can be planned in the villages for collection of night soil for feeding to biogas plants. Wastes of 200 persons can be used to product about 5 m^3 of gas per day to extract 12 kWh of equivalent energy by running a biogas engine.

3.5 BIOMASS GASIFIERS

The estimated production of agricultural residues in India is 200 million tonnes per year compared to about 130 million tonnes of wood. In equivalent energy content, this amounts to about 54 million tonnes of coal which is 50 percent of our annual coal production of 108 million tonnes in the country. Of this total residue, about 40 million tonnes is used in commercial sector, the remaining is burnt in fields, used for fodder, roofing material, for composting and other needs. It appears that a substantial amount of residue is available as fuel.

The direct burning of biogas in domestic hearths is grossly inefficient, giving only 8 to 11 percent useful energy. Biomass residues because of their low bulk density and extensive smoke formation are the most inconvenient and pollutant fuel. It is therefore, desirable to use biomass more efficiently.

Gasifier is essencially a thermochemical reactor in which the biomass undergoes partial oxidation and producer gas is obtained. The agricultural and forest residues can first be dried in solar driers to restrict the moisture content below 15 percent. These are pressed in compaction briquetting machines to prepare feed size of 50–70 mm for the gasifier. The biomass briquets are ignited in the gasifier and air flow is controlled to ensure partial combustion. The producer gas is reduced to CO and H_2 by carbon present in the burnt layers. The main constituents of fuel gas are CO, H_2 and CH_4.

The gas produced by the gasifier is hot and contains tar, vapours and soot particles. To make it engineworthy, it is cooled to near ambient condition and cleaned to remove tar and dust by cross-current water scrubbers. Air and clean gas are supplied to the engine in per-specified proportions. On an average 1 kg of biomass produces 2.5 nm^3 of fuel gas and 1 kWh of shaft energy to drive the irrigation pump.

The diesel engine utilizes the gas as a supplementary fuel operating on duel-fuel mode. The solar driers, briquetting machines and gasifies are now made in India. The total cost of a biomass gasifier with gas cooler and scrubber of

15 m^3/hr capacity, 5 kW/1500 rpm diesel engine and 100 × 100 mm centrifugal pump with necessary controls and accessories is about ₹ 37,500.

3.6 HYDRAULIC RAMS

The utilization of hydroenergy to operate agricultural and industrial devices is one of the oldest and wide spread techniques of human achievements, Hydraulic rams manufactured by John Blank Ltd., UK was installed at Taj Mahal, Agra in 1900 for raising water from the Yamuna at the rate of 2700 m^3 per day. It is still working satisfactorily with very low maintenance cost. Blake Hydrams installed at Risalpur (Pakistan) in 1925 raise 4869 m^3 of water per day to a vertical height of 20 m and to a horizontal distance of 1600 m. Hydraulic rams are also used in the Alpine areas of the world for the water supply of remote farms for irrigation and drinking water purposes.

Hydraulic ram is a contrivance to raise a part of large amount of water available at some height, to a greater height. This is employed when some natural source of water like a spring or a stream is available at some altitude, *e.g.*, in a hilly region. Work done by a large quantity of water in falling through a small height is used to raise a small part of it to a greater height. Action of water hammer makes it feasible. No external power is, therefore, required to work this machine. Other attractions are: negligible amount of maintenance and supervision costs, continuous operation, high efficiency, quite operation and possibility of automatic adjustment of water supply. The liftable volume of water diminishes asymtotically with lifting height. In case of medium lifting heights, the hydraulic ram operates with an efficiency absolutely comparable to a piston pump of the same performance.

As the hydraulic ram does not need a driving unit, it is to be considered as ideal for hilly areas, where the supply in fossil energy carriers or electricity is problematic. The hydraulic ram operates with water streams of 1 to 40 m^3/s and fall heads of 1.5 to 30 m and with lifting heights up to 300 m, which means an efficiency in the range of about 50 percent to 2 percent at the minimum. There is a number of different types which can be distinguished by the operation of the oscillating valves.

Hydraulic ram is a simple and rugged device for operating irrigation schemes and deserves R & D inputs for its performance improvement and adoption to irrigation.

3.7 WATER MILLS

Poncelet water wheel or a Darrieus Turbine Rotor can be sumberged in a river, water stream or canal to tap current energy from water speeds as low as 1 m/s. The mechanical energy thus obtained is used for driving irrigation pumps. The blends of water mills can be made from fabricated steel, ferrocement, glass fibre or timber depending upon the availability of local materials and skills. The power output depends upon the swept area and cube of water velocity. A vertical axis rotor of 3.75 m^2 swept area runs at 13.5 rpm in 1 m/s current velocity. From this, a belt drives a pulley on an intermediate shaft which rotates at about 110 rpm and from this shaft another belt drives a centrifugal pump mounted on the pontoon at approximately 950 rpm. A 50 mm floating pipeline is connected to the pump to lift water from the river. In a current speed of 1.18 m/s, it lifts 3.51/s of water against a vertical height of 5 m and horizontal distánce of 25 m and can be used to irrigate a one or two hectare riverside horticultural plot.

Although the machine will work at lower speeds, it is unlikely to be economical proposition in a current speed below 1 m/s. The energy available in river current increases with cube of water velocity; a two-fold increase in water velocity has an energy flux eight times greater.

3.8 CONCLUSIONS

The bulk of future energy needs of India are not going to be met by fossil fuels and hydroelectric plants alone and have to be met from a variety of sources. Similarly, geographical conditions dictate the exploitation of locally available energy sources for lift irrigation utilising the appropriate intermediate technologies to convert them to mechanical energy for driving irrigation pumps. Some of the sources and technologies immediately available for this purpose have been discussed. An all out effort is needed to upgrade the performance of these services and for adopting them to irrigation schemes. Special attention must be paid to the development and adoption of hydraulic rams and water mills for irrigation schemes which have relatively lacked behind.

3.9 REFERENCES

1. Singal, R.K., '*Floating Type Micro Hydro Power Plants*', Electrical India, Bombay, 30th September 1984.
2. Daniel M. Simmons, '*Wind Power*', Noyes Data Corporation, Park Ridge, New Jersey, 1975.
3. Nirmal K. Pande, '*Energy Constraints—Need to Tap Renewable Sources*', Economic Times, July 5, 1984.
4. A.A.M. Sayigh, '*Solar Energy Engineering*', Academic Press, London, 1971.
5. Singal, R.K., "*Non-Conventional Energy for Lift Irrigation*", Electrical India, March, 1985.

PART 2
MANPOWER DEVELOPMENT

Special Course in Rural Technology

Chapter 4

4.1 INTRODUCTION

The usefulness of an education system depends upon its relevance to the social and economic environment. There is hardly any place in our curricula and syllabi of our engineering courses for rural industries, transport, agricultural practice, rural forestry, irrigation needs, building materials, housing and other rural development programmes which touch the lives of 76 percent of our population. These deficiencies and distortions in our engineering education can be rectified by introducing an integrated engineering course in Rural Technology.

This Chapter proposes the design of a course at degree level in Rural Technology which includes the course contents, methodology of teaching and evaluation so that education can be fully integrated with rural development. The students are expected to be exposed to live rural situations and village problems and will be trained to solve them using appropriate technologies and management techniques. The students will earn and receive suitable compensation for the services rendered by them so that their output are of professional standards.

In a country of 5,76,276 villages, Rural Technology graduates will not only transform the lives of rural population but the scheme will be useful and a very powerful source of employment generation for the technically educated manpower.

4.2 COURSE CONTENTS

The curriculum of the Under-graduate Programme is so designed that the successful graduates of this course in Rural Technology would be well equiped for employment or self-employment in rural areas to exploit the rural resources for economic and social development of rural population through technology and management techniques. The course has been designed as an eight semester programme of equal credits spread over four years and covers various disciplines of engineering and management as relevant to rural development. The broad division on credit rating is given below:

Engineering Sciences	: 18 credit units
Construction Engineering	: 37 credit units
Mechanical Engineering	: 42 credit units
Electrical, electronics and computer engineering	: 45 credit units
Food, agriculture, irrigation and chemical engineering	: 22 credit units
Industry and management	: 32 credit units
Practical Training/projects	: 44 credit units
Total	: 240 credit units.

The course contents are specially designed for the Integrated course for rural development. The detailed Schedule of Course to be offered for the B.Tech. Degree in Rural Technology is enclosed as Annexure-I.

4.3 TEACHING METHODOLOGY

Variety of class-room techniques and training methods should be used to make learning purposeful and productive. Extensive range of Audio-visual equipment should be used in the lecture sessions. Specially prepared video films of half-an-hour duration for lecture sessions should be followed by intensive discussions to ensure active participation by the students.

Case Method should be used to inculcate in the student, capability to analyse, select problems and to develop analytical thinking and rational approach to problem solving.

Training methods should also include syndicate discussions and working sessions. The faculty should be drawn from various basic disciplines, having diverse experience in design, industry, business and Government in variety of functional areas and should be able to bring to bear academic concepts to practical problems. Practising engineers and executives should be invited for special lectures complement the full-time faculty. Management games should be played to simulate real-life environment demanding active involvement and participation.

The training and project work should be carried out in selected villages and industrial units for solving live rural problems. The students should be associated with practising engineers and managers engaged in rural projects and they should be paid suitable compensation so that their outputs are of professional standards. The programme should thus be knowledge centered, application oriented and a source of earning for the students.

4.4 FACILITIES

The library should have Technical books, Dictionaries, Encyclopedias, Handbooks, Manuals, Workbooks. It should have video based and self-learning modules and TV studio multi-media expertise in the development of special video-based self-learning modules.

The Computer Center should be equipped with hard disk based super mini computer system, PCs with System and Application Software, draftsman package and plotter.

The workshop should have facilities for machine shop, welding, carpentary, casting, forging repair technologies and prototype development and testing. The laboratories should be equipped with state-of-art technology pilot plants relevant to rural application.

Special projection rooms and seminar halls should be provided with audio-video systems.

4.5 TRAINING AND PROJECTS

Special emphasis should be placed on training and project work to ensure students' participation in rural projects and problem solving. Nearly 20 percent time has been reserved for training and project work in the form of six slots, one nearly in each semester. The students are expected to be exposed to live rural situations and village problems and should be trained by the practising engineers and executives to solve them by using appropriate technologies and management techniques. The students should learn and earn suitable compensation for the services rendered by them in the execution of actual projects in progress.

4.6 CONCLUSIONS

It is expected that Rural Technology graduates will play a very important role towards rural development. There is need of large number of such engineers and managers who can be involved in planning and exploiting the local resources available in the 576276 villages in the country for transforming the lives of rural population forming 76 percent of our total people in the country. Only through such engineers specially trained for rural development can the Governmental rural development programmes be meaningfully implemented for achieving desired results.

The overall rural development is possible only through large number of rural industries, mechanization of agriculture, food harvesting and preservation, food processing, etc. There is a need for a very large number of Rural Technologists for the planning, execution and control of such projects and programmes.

ANNEXURE-1

SCHEDULE OF COURSES TO BE OFFERED FOR B. TECH. DEGREE IN RURAL TECHNOLOGY

SEMESTER	CODE NO.	TITLE	CREDITS
I	S – 101	Engineering Mathematics	4
	S – 102	Engineering Physics	4
	S – 103	Engineering Chemistry	4
	C – 101	Engineering Drawing	4
	C – 102	Surveying	4
	M – 101	Manufacturing and Repair Practices	4
	S – 110	Engineering Mathematics [P]	2
	S – 111	Engineering Physics [P]	2
	S – 112	Engineering Chemistry [P]	2
		Total	30
II	M – 201	Machine Drawing	4
	C – 201	Elements of Civil Engg.	3
	E – 201	Elements of Electrical Engg.	3
	CH – 201	Elements of Chemical Engg.	4
	A – 201	Elements of Agriculture Engg.	4
	C – 202	Public Health, Sanitation and Domestic Water Supply	4
	M – 210	Workshop Practice [P]	4
	C – 210	Surveying [P]	4
		Total	30
III	M – 301	Elements of Mechanical Engg.	4
	EC – 301	Elements of Electronic Engg.	4
	Co – 301	Elements of Computer Engg.	4
	S – 301	Organisation Behaviour and Communication	4
	A – 301	Animal Husbandry and Dairy Engineering	4
	C – 310	Civil Engg. Laboratory	2
	E – 310	Electrical Engg. Laboratory	2
	M – 310	Mechanical Engg. Laboratory	2
	T – 310	Practical Training	4
		Total	30
IV	E – 401	Electrical Network and Distribution Systems	4
	C – 401	Water Resource Management and Irrigation Schemes	4
	C – 402	Village Planning and Road Construction	4
	M – 401	Farm Machinery, Agricultural Pumps and Automobile Engg.	4

	Ec – 401	Control Engg. and Instruments	4
	Co – 401	Database Management Systems and Software Engg.	4
	Co – 410	Computer Programming [P]	2
	Ec – 410	Electronics Engg. Laboratory	2
	Ch – 410	Chemical Engg. Laboratory	2
		Total	30
V	M – 501	Engineering Materials	4
	M – 502	Food Processing, Cottage and Rural Industries	4
	M – 503	Mechanised Agriculture	4
	C – 501	Architecture, Structural Design and Materials for Low cost housing	4
	C – 502	Environmental Engg.	4
	S – 501	Engineering and Managerial Economics	4
	T – 510	Winter Project	6
		Total	30
VI	M – 601	Maintenance Engg. and Management	4
	M – 602	Food Preservation, Cold Storage and Refrigeration	4
	E – 601	Repair and Maintenance of Electrical Equipment and Systems	4
	Ec – 601	Telecommunications	4
	Co – 601	Computer Applications in Rural Systems	4
	T – 610	Summer Project	10
		Total	30
VII	I-701	Rural Facilities Planning	4
	I-702	Entrepreneurship	4
	I-703	Systems Approach to Problem Solving and Decision Making	4
	M-701	Rural Energy Sources and Power Supply Systems	4
	I-704	Human Factor Engg.	4
	T-701	Minor Project	10
		Total	30
VIII	M-801	Rural Energy Technologies and Rural Development Programmes	4
	I-801	Project Engg. and Management	4
	I-802	Rural Resource Management	4
	I-803	Management of Small Scale Industries	4
	T-810	Final Project	14
		Total	30

Part 3
Solar Energy

Chapter 5

Solar Energy and its Rural Applications

5.1 INTRODUCTION

The energy consumption from Christ birth to 1750 AD has been estimated as 2.34 × 10^{15} kWh; from 1800 AD to 1900 AD, 1.17 × 10^{15} kWh and during the period 2000 AD to 2100 AD, it may be anything from 29.3 × 10^{15} kWh to 117 × 10^{15} kWh due to increase in world population and man's standard of living. This may fall short of total world resources of fossil fuels, estimates of which are given in Table 5.1.

Table 5.1 World Resources in Fossil Fuels

Coal	:	5.27 × 10^{15} kWh
Natural gas	:	0.618 × 10^{15} kWh
Oil	:	0.996 × 10^{15} kWh
Uranium	:	23.4 × 10^{15} kWh
Thorium	:	14.0 × 10^{15} kWh
Total	:	44.28 × 10^{15} kWh

The rate of production of a non renewable energy resource increases with time, reaches a maximum, and then decays. The peaking indicates that the end of its availability is in sight and alternate source of energy must become increasingly available to meet the growing energy requirements. According to present estimates, about 88 percent of the world's fossil fuels (excluding nuclear fuels) is coal. There is a reasonable agreement among various investigators that the peaking time of coal falls somewhere about the year 2040. It takes somewhere between 20 to 40 years for a new technology to come to fruition and it is therefore, prudent to plan for shifting a major share of the total world energy production from fossil fuels to some other plentiful sources by no later than the end of this century.

The following new and renewable sources of energy have been identified at NRSE Conference under UN, held in Nairobi in 1981:

1. Solar energy	2. Wind energy
3. Hydro energy	4. Biomass (Wastes)
5. Tidal energy	6. Thermal gradients in Oceans
7. Waves	8. Geothermal
9. Firewood	10. Charcoal
11. Draught Animals	12. Peat (Raw coal)
13. Oil Shale (Oil in rocks)	14. Tar sand

Of all the currently known available sources, only nuclear and solar energy have the potential of supplying large amounts of power within the available time frame. These two sources have to complement each other to meet the demand economically and safely.

Solar energy is an essentially inexhaustible source potentially capable of meeting significant portion of the worlds future energy needs with a minimum of adverse environmental consequences. There appears to be a general agreement that solar energy is the most promising of the unconventional energy sources. However, considerable technical and economic problems must be solved before any large scale utilization of solar energy can occur. Science, technology, economics, sociology, and politics will play a part in the development and utilization of solar energy on a large scale. This Chapter highlights the special properties of solar energy and its potential applications under Indian conditions.

5.2 AVAILABILITY OF SOLAR ENERGY

Solar energy has received the greatest attention during the decade of the 1970s. Many regarded it as the solution for reducing the use of fossil and nuclear fuels and eventually replacing all current means of production of both electric-power and thermal energy requirements. Solar energy, in sheer size, does have the potential to supply all energy, needs: electric, thermal, process, and chemical, and even transportation fuels.

The sun is a sphere of intensely hot gaseous matter, continuously generating heat by thermonuclear fusion reactions converting hydrogen atoms into helium atoms. This energy is radiated from the sun in all directions and a very small fraction of it reaches on the earth. The earth and its atmosphere receive continuously 1.7×10^{17} W of radiations from the sun. A world population of 10 billion with a total power need per person of 10 kW would require about 10^{11} kW of energy. It is thus apparent that if irradiance on only one percent of the earth's surface could be converted into useful energy with 10 percent efficiency, solar energy could fulfil the energy needs of the entire population.

The immense magnitude of direct solar energy can be illustrated by the following estimates. The average solar constant at sea level is 1 kW/m^2. As the normal surface of the earth presented to the sun is πR^2 where R is the radius of the earth, the total solar energy at sea level is approximately:

$$1\ \text{kW/m}^2 \times \pi \times (3960\ \text{miles})^2 \times (1610\ \text{m/mile})^2 = 1.28\ \text{kW} \times 10^{14}.$$

If 1 percent of the earth's surface is used for converting solar energy into useful energy at an efficiency of 10 percent (a figure well below that of some available solar cells), the useful energy generated per year is:

$$1.28 \times 10^{14}\ \text{kW} \times 0.01 \times 0.1 \times 24 \times 365 = 11.2 \times 10^{14}\ \text{kWh}.$$

This is the present annual rate of consumption of the whole world. Another interesting comparison is that the total fossil energy on earth is less than the solar energy incident upon the earth in one year.

Solar energy is however, very diffuse, cyclic and often undependable. It, therefore, needs systems and components that can gather and concentrate it efficiently for conversion to any of these uses and that can do the conversion as efficiently as possible.

5.3 COLLECTION OF SOLAR ENERGY

The mean extra-terrestrial irradiance, normal to the solar beam on the other fringes of the earth's atmosphere is approximately 1.35 kW/m^2. This varies by + 3.4 percent during the year due to elliptical orbit of the earth. The radiant energy from the sun is distributed over a range of wavelengths and can be approximated by the spectrum of a black body at 5800 K. The amount of irradiance is reduced and solar spectrum is substantially modified in passing through the earth's atmosphere, and approximately 25–50 percent of its energy is lost by scattering and absorption.

The solar energy resource can be divided into natural and technological collection systems. Further sub-division of these are shown in Fig. 5.1.

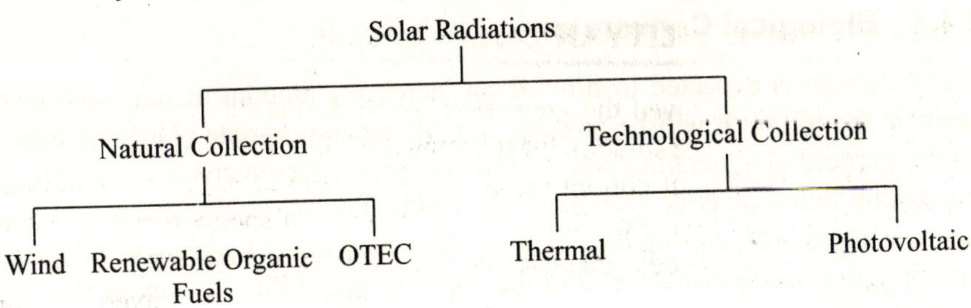

Fig. 5.1

5.4 CONVERSION SYSTEMS

5.4.1 Thermal Conversion

Solar energy collectors consist of a dark surface facing the sun. It absorbs solar energy and heats up. Part of the absorbed energy is transferred to a working fluid in contact with it. One or two sheets of glass are usually placed over the absorber surface to reduce the heat losses due to the radiation and convection. Improvements such as the use of selective surfaces, evacuation of the collector to reduce heat losses, and special kinds of glasses are used to increase the efficiency of the devices. These flat plate collectors are available for operation over a range of temperature upto approx. 365 K for producing hot water, space heating and operation of absórber type air-conditioning systems. This thermal low-temperature utilization is also economically attractive.

Operating temperatures as high as 4000 K have been achieved by the use of focussing devices for solar furnaces. Generation of steam to operate pumps for irrigation purposes and conventional steam engines for generation of electricity has also proved technologically feasible. The cost of solar power in favourable locations will be compatible with that of nuclear power when the development of these plants have been completed.

5.4.2 Photovoltaic Conversion

Photovoltaic solar cells utilize energetic photóns of the incident solar radiations directly to produce electricity at high conversion efficiencies of about 24 percent (theoretical) and 15 percent (achieved). The technology of photovoltaic conversion is well developed as a part of satellite and space-travel technology but large scale application is hampered by the high price of photocells which is about 100 times more than electric energy from conventional fossil – and nuclear-fuel electric power plants. A cost reduction of the order of 100 to 1 will be necessary before photovoltaic conversion can be economically viable. Efforts to reduce the production costs of solar cells are directed towards drawing thin monocrystalline materials, development of concentrating devices to reduce surface areas of solar cells required and the highly innovative fabrication techniques.

5.4.3 Biological Conversion

Bioconversion is expected to provide an increasing amount of our total energy needs in the future. It will be possible to cultivate appropriate plants exclusively for the purpose of generating power either by direct bioconversion or by pyrolytic conversion into liquids or gaseous fuels. Cultivation of special plants like sugar cane can improve the conversion efficiency from the present 1 percent to 2.5 percent. The recycling processes are within the realm of possibility to convert the waste products of food and animals to methane and methanol.

5.4.4 Wind Power

The technology of wind power production is well developed and cost estimates in favourable regions of the world are fairly close to those of other energy sources. Rotor diameters of 50 m and heights of 100 m are dimensions typically for wind generation to produce appreciable amount of power. The unreliability of power production due to large variability in wind velocity has hamphered the large scale applications even in favourable regions.

5.4.5 Solar Energy Conversion by Oceans

Oceans forming almost 71 percent of the world's surface serve as a tremendous storehouse of solar energy due to the temperature differences produced by the sun as well as kinetic energy stored in the waves. There are a number of places in the ocean where temperature differences of the order of 20–25 K exist at depths of less than 1000 m, and these temperature differences could be used to operate low pressure heat engines. Although the thermodynamic efficiencies are low, the available amount of thermal energy is very large. The cost of using the temperature gradients in the ocean for practical solar energy utilization depends largely on the development of efficient and cheap heat exchangers which form the bulk of the plant cost.

At present only the thermal method is sufficiently advanced to compete economically with other sources, including nuclear. A large amount of suitable materials and workforce as well as proper level of technology will be required if one-quarter of all the energy requirement of the world were to be provided by thermal conversion of solar energy by 2020. The contribution of various conversion methods discussed above to useful energy needs of the world supplied by solar energy by 2020 are projected below:

Solar Technology	*Percent Contribution*
I. Direct thermal applications:	
1. Heating and cooling	30
2. Agricultural applications	6
3. Industrial applications	4
	40
II. Solar Electric capacity:	
1. Wind	7
2. Photovoltaic	10
3. Solar thermal	8
4. Ocean thermal	5
	30
III. Fuels from biomass	30
	100

5.5 LIMITATIONS OF SOLAR ENERGY

The nature of solar energy source has certain limitations which affect the engineering design of the equipment and system and reduces its cost effectiveness.

5.5.1 Low Flux Density

Large surfaces are needed to collect solar energy of low flux density for large-scale utilization resulting in an increased cost of the delivered energy. When the sun is directly overhead on a cloudless day, 10 m^2 of surface could theoretically provide energy at 10 percent efficiency of collection at the rate of 1 kW. Most of the manmade solar collectors can convert only direct energy efficiently and the position of the sun, thick clouds and anthropogenic pollution let less energy pass and scatter the energy back into space and percentage of diffuse energy increases. Almost total absorption of solar energy by ozone at wavelengths below 300 nm and by carbondioxide at wavelengths beyond 2500 nm, the irradiance on the earth's surface is effectively limited to wavelengths between 300 to 2500 nm. In that range the solar energy is used selectively by different processes given below:

	Process	Useable Wavelength Range (nm)
1.	Thermal conversion	300–2500
2.	Solar cells	300–1200
3.	Photochemistry	300–1000
4.	Photobiology (Photosynthesis)	400–700

5.5.2 Intermittency of Solar Energy

Solar energy has a regular daily cycle due to the turning of the earth around its axis, a regular annual cycle due to inclination of the earth axis with the plane of the elliptic and due to the motion of the earth around the sun, and is also unavailable during periods of bad weather. The diffuse and cyclic nature of the source introduce special problems in storage and distribution of the energy, restrict the areas of application and need supplementation from other sources.

5.5.3 Global Distribution of Solar Energy

The global distribution of solar energy does not favour the industrial parts of the world, but may be of help to industrially developing countries located in the favourable radiation belt. The greatest amount of energy is available in the continent deserts areas around 25°N and 25°S of the equator and falls off towards both the equator and the poles. Mostly these are flat deserts that are practically unuseable for agriculture or any kind of industrial development. These regions have little or no water which can create special problems in the generation of thermal electric power.

The mean annual horizontal surface irradiance for India is about 200 W/m^2 and for Thar desert it exceeds 250 W/m^2.

5.5.4 Cost Effectiveness

Although solar energy is essentially free, there is definite cost effectiveness associated with its utilization. Whereas for conventional energy sources, the processing cost has traditionally been borne by large industries which borrow money from a bank and then charge the consumer for each unit of energy used. Solar energy installations, especially for low temperature application in home heating and cooling, are the total responsibility of the user. As a result of this shift in the economic risk a solar energy installation appears to the users as a huge additional investment that they personally must make in advance before deriving any benefit from it. Solar energy must be viewed as a long-term investment, and its cost must be prorated just like cost of fossil fuels. Acceptance of this view is necessary to assess the cost effectiveness of solar energy.

5.5.5 Energy Intensive

Much of the construction materials used for collecting and converting solar radiation, whether thermal or photovoltaic are themselves very energy intensive. For example, large quantities of aluminium, steel, copper, concrete, glass and plastic are needed, all of which require large quantities of energy for conversion from ore to finished products. The photovoltaic conversion requires the extremely energy intensive processing of sand to crystalline silican. The energy consumed in the processes for producing the above finished products and in constructing the systems is a large fraction of the net energy generated during the life of the plant. This fraction is in most cases bordering on the unacceptable limits, except in special cases where solar energy is uniquely suited.

5.5.6 Environmental Pollution

Solar energy systems are not pollution free as usually expected. The mining of large quantities of mineral ores, the processing of these ores to the finished material, the manufacturing of the equipment, and construction of the plants are processes that generate their own pollution and health and occupational safety risks. In addition, the low efficiency of these plants, whether thermal or photovoltaic, results in large heat-rejection plants, hence, the thermal pollution.

5.6 APPLICATIONS

Most developing countries including India are located in those regions of the world (between 35°N and 35°S) which are most blessed with sun-shine. The relative high population densities in the rural areas in these regions, and the high exposure to the sun therefore make it natural that the applications of solar energy, which lends itself to decentralized power of small size, should be given high priority when trying to solve the energy problems in the developing countries.

Although solar energy may be used in many markets, such as in active and passive space heating and cooling, industrial process heating, desalination and water heating and in electric generation where power requirements are small and in remote areas, we are concerned to find applications of solar energy most suited to Indian conditions.

5.6.1 Indian Situation

India is bestowed with plentiful of sunshine for 250–300 days per year. In south and central India, the annual average daily incidence of solar energy is about 4.5 kWh/m^2 with the maximum exceeding even 7.0 kWh/m^2. Therefore, solar energy offers an attractive solution to some of the energy problems in India.

India is essentially an agricultural country with 78 percent of its population living in rural villages and 70 percent of its gross domestic product emanating from the rural agricultural sector. Population-wise the distribution of villages is as shown blow:

Population	*No. of Villages*	*Percentage of Total*
Up to 499	349,995	62.2
500 to 999	118,602	21.0
1,000 to 1999	65,101	11.6
2,000 to 4999	26,400	4.6
5,000 to 9999	3,404	0.6
10,000 and above	744	0.2
Total	564,276	100.0

About 95 percent of these villages are small with a population of less than 2000. On average, these villages consume 150 kWh of energy per day for energising irrigation pumps, for lighting, for cooking, etc. As the load factor is very low and because these villages are widely dispersed, it is most uneconomical to electrify them from power grids. Transportation of commercial fuels like coal, diesel and petrol over long distances is very difficult and transmission and distribution of electricity through power grids to far flung areas are prohibitably expensive. The farmers and craftmen are not in a position to pay for high costs of energy thus small scale industries in rural areas are reduced and there are limited irrigation possibilities in agriculture. There is a continuous flux of population to new economic centres which has created the problem of mushrooming of slums and destructions of social life. These problems can explode with very serious consequences. The population migration must be checked by creating opportunities in rural areas. The development, welfare and prosperity of rural villages depend upon the availability of cheap and abundant energy for domestic cooking, heating and lighting, community development, irrigation water, mechanised agriculture and small industrial parks, based on local resources. Solar energy and other locally available energy sources must be utilized to boost the agricultural production which is vitally important to raise the standard of living of growing population.

If the energy and power needs of the villages can be met from local sources, the central/zonal power grids connecting coal based thermal power plants, nuclear and hydro-plants can work in more efficient and reliable manner at high load factors feeding power only to industrial belts and big commercial centres. Tremendous investments and huge power losses in the long and unwieldy power lines to remote and scatterd villages can be saved.

In the light of the above situation, there is an urgent need to the use/development of the following solar appliances for rural villages:

(*i*) Solar cookers which must fit well with the age-old habits of the conventional cooking and should be accepted by the rural population in India without any reservations.

(*ii*) Small solar driven refrigeration units for preservation of food, storage of milk and other products in rural areas where little electric power is available.

(*iii*) Solar water irrigation pumps to boost the agricultural production which is vitally important in view of growing population.

(*iv*) Solar water heaters and dryers for agricultural products.

(*v*) Small power plants to produce electricity for domestic and street lighting and cottage industries.

Some studies and design work has been undertaken at Regional Engineering College, Kurukshetra to boost the development work and utilization of solar energy in the above fields.

5.6.2 Specific Applications: Hot Plate Type Solar Cooker

Eighty percent of the basic energy needs of rural India is the provision of cooking energy, which amounts to 0.5 to 1 kWh/person/day with a peak power of 0.2 to 1.2 kW per capita. It is mostly met from traditional fuels like fire-wood and cowdung cakes. The Government of India is trying to introduce box-type solar cookers with financial subsidies with poor success due to many technical drawbacks of the design. The temperature obtained is less than 100°C and is insufficient for chapati making and frying which are very important cooking processes. There is no provision for storage of heat and cooking has to be carried out while the sun is shining which is an odd time for preparing dinner and breakfast. Cooking has to be carried out in the open without privacy and in the sun which is very inconvenient to the housewife. In order to overcome these difficulties, a small family size solar cooker was designed and fabricated at REC, Kurukshetra. It consists of a flat plate with mirror boosters. It is coupled to an oil storage insulated tank placed under the cooking platform inside the kitchen through a thermosyphon to the outside collector. It can provide sufficient flux of heat energy at high enough temperature to a hot plate through a heat pipe. The system would be suitable for cooking of conventional foods at convenient time for breakfast, lunch and dinner inside the kitchen. It would just replace a bottled gas cooking range and would be fitted permanently. It will fit in with the age-old habits and practices of rural households.

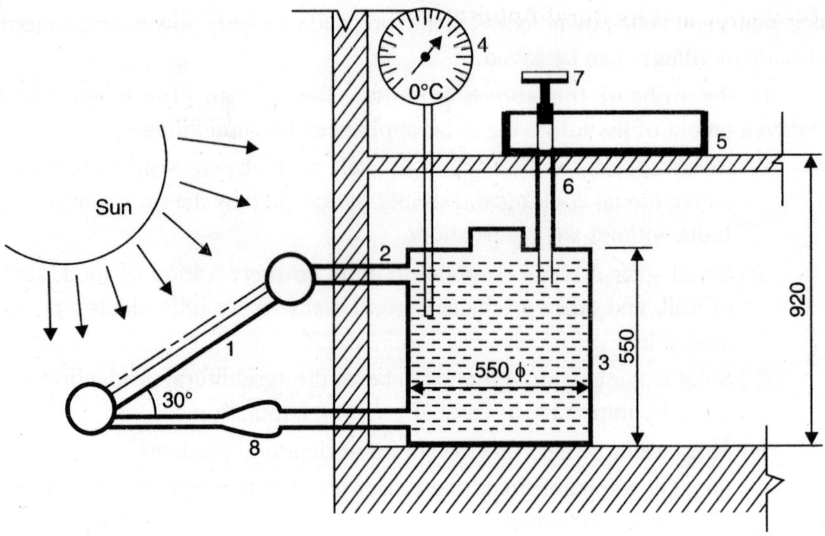

1. Solar collector (1 m²)
2. Thermosyphon (1½″ NB)
3. Hot oil storage tank (100 l)
4. Thermometer (0–300°C)
5. Hot plate (2 kW)
6. Heat pipe (2 kW)
7. Control valve
8. Non-return valve

Fig. 5.2 Flow diagram of hot-plate-type solar cooker

It is coupled to a thermal storage system and can last for a day without sunshine. The heat flux rate can be conveniently controlled by turning a small control valve suitably placed at the hot plate. There are no operating and maintenance expenses and lifelong oil fill is provided. The prototype cost of ₹ 3000 can be substantially reduced during commercial design and manufacture.

5.6.3 Solar Refrigerator

At the 1975 UNESCO conference on solar energy several developing countries stated that small solar driven units are urgently needed for preservation of food in rural areas where little electric power is available. A study and design project was undertaken at REC, Kurukshetra for the development of refrigeration cycle was adopted because of absence of moving parts, toxic and corrosive chemicals and expectation of long and troublefree operation life, a small solar refrigerator, Solid absorption-Zeolite. It was sized for fitting onto the cabinet of the present 165L capacity domestic refrigerator. It consists of a 1.5 m^2 flat plate collector filled with 50 mm thick zeolite. Water vapour is driven out of collector by solar heating during the day. The vapour are condensed and stored in a tank until evening. As the collector cools at night due to the sky radiation, a vacuum in the system causes the water in the evaporator to boil constantly at a temperature of –2°C at a pressure of 4 mm of Hg. The frozen surface can make 9 kg of ice in 8 hours. The water vapours returns to the collector for reabsorption into zeolite and the system is ready for the next day. The ice can be removed for use or left to cool the refrigerator at times of no sunshine.

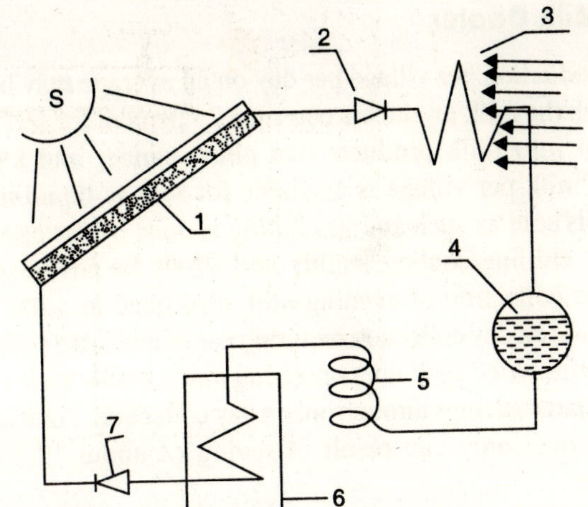

1. 1.5 m^2 Zeolite filled solar collector.
2. 10 NB Non-return valve (Ball type).
3. 4.2 m^2 Panel coil condenser.
4. 20 L Water storage tank.
5. 0.5 mm X 1.4 m Capillary tube.
6. 0.3 m^2 Panel coil evaporator and ice tank.
7. 32 NB Non-return valve (Ball type).

Fig. 5.3 Flow diagram

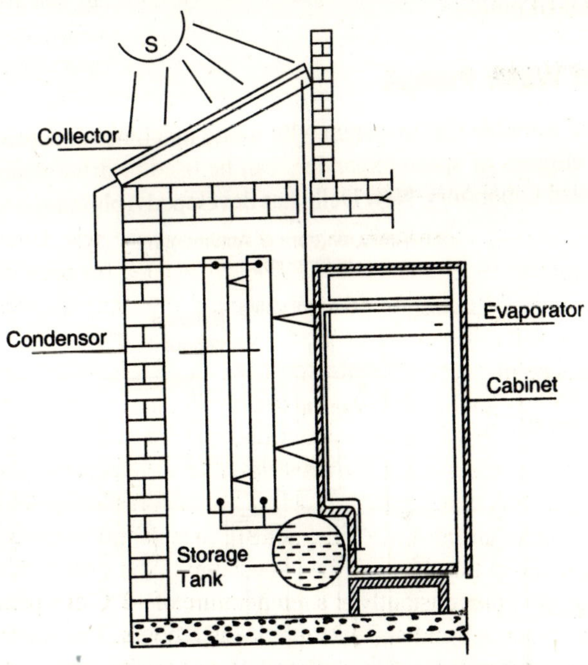

Fig. 5.4 Arrangement drawing of refrigerator

The project experience can be used to develope small cold storages for preservation of food in rural areas.

5.6.4 Solar Milk Cooler

The total milk production per village per day on an average may be taken as 2000 litres; out of which the milk producers consume 25 percent for self use and convert about 45 percent into milk products like ghee, paneer and khoa. Therefore, 500/600 litres of milk per village is available for sale as liquid milk per day. At present this milk is sold as such and its chilling is done by the agencies procuring it. A village-level chilling/cooling facility will surely be advantageous as it will make possible the collection of evening milk also once in a day which is more economical than twice a day collection requiring use of available collection, transport and chilling facilities twice each time operating much below their rated capacities. There will thus be large savings through once a day collection. For example reduction in route kilometerage only can result in saving of about 12.5 percent of the procurement price.

Rural processing of milk can add value to the product and increase rural income. The zeolite solar refrigerator system can be attached to a cooling-cum-storeage tank made of single-embossed panel coils of stainless steel, the inside being plain sheet and outside made of embossed sheet. The water refrigerant circulates by thermosyphon effect in the walls and acts as a very efficient heat exchanger thus reducing the temperature difference between milk and water vapour to less than 0.5°C. As water storage is in the bottom, it makes possible to cool even small quantities of milk.

5.6.5 Solar Water Pumps

Organic vapour Rankine Cycle system with rotary machines or screw expanders or reciprocating engines or spiral expanders can be used to drive water pumps. The National Physical Laboratory, New Delhi has developed Abhimanyu Solar Pump of

Schematic diagram of Abhimanyu solar pump

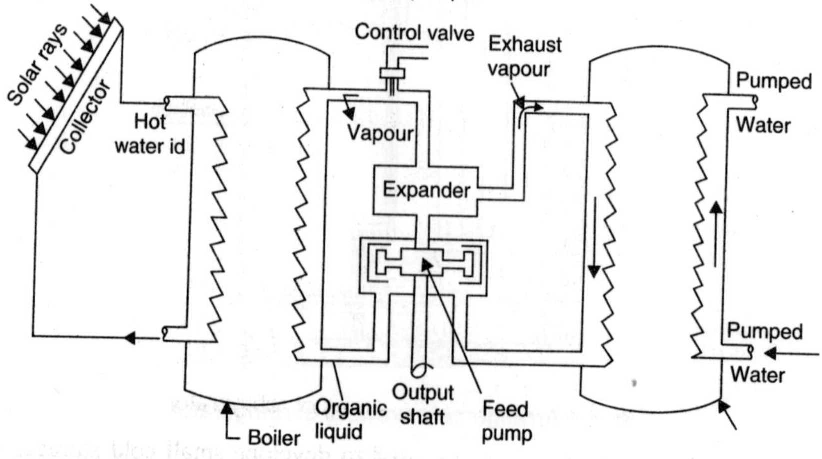

Fig. 5.5

1 kW rating using R114. An area of 10 m^2 is used to operate the pump for 4 hours a day. When not pumping, it can be used to drive a generator or thresher or a lathe. The total cost of the components (condenser, boiler, expansion motor, storage tank, collector assembly and pump) is ₹ 12500 and if we include the development charges, overheads and labour for assembly, the total cost will be of the order of ₹ 37000.

The Central Electronics Ltd. Sahidabad (UP) have developed a solar photo voltaic water pumping system with the following specifications:

Solar Panel: 300 W (peak). 2.4 × 2.5 m (size)

System Voltage: 60 V DC nominal

Motor Pump Set: DC Motor-centrifugal pump monoblok.

Capacity: 30 to 40 m^3 per day at 5 m total head.

The total cost of the system including solar photovoltaic array, on/off switch, motor pump set, accessories including suction and delivery valves and piping is about ₹ 40000 which is highly subsidised and installed at a cost of ₹ 5000 only for a small or marginal farmer.

5.6.6 Hybrid Energy System

Solar energy can be integrated with other energy resources locally available for meeting the total energy and power requirements. Depending upon the location, the other resources of the village which can be exploited are:

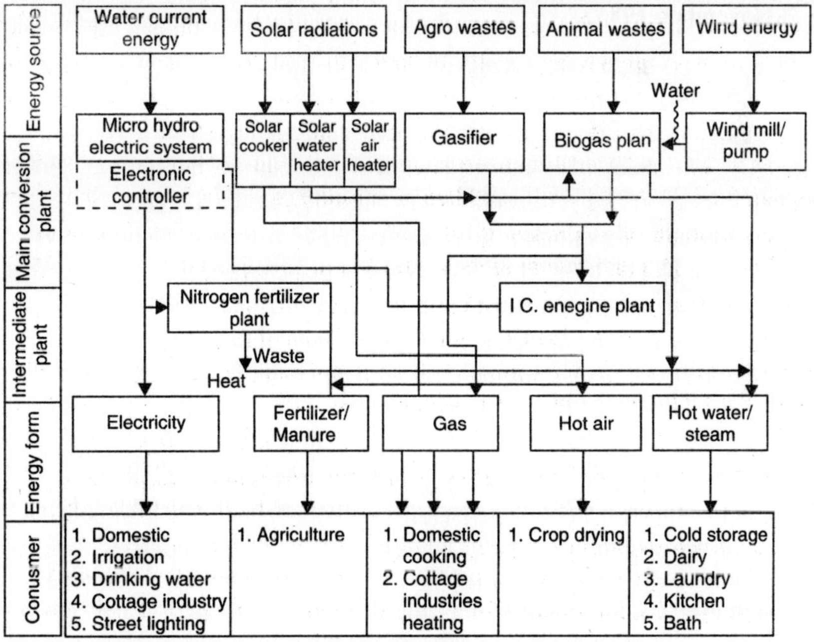

Hybrid Energy System

Fig. 5.6

- Water current energy in the rivers and irrigation canals where micro hydro power plants working on low head or zero head turbines can be installed for generation of electric power.
- Biomass for generation of power by direct burning in fluidised bed combustors for generation of steam for a turbine or production of fuel gas by gasification and running an I.C. Engine plant.
- Animal wastes for generation of biogas for running an I.C. Engine or cooking gas.
- Wind energy for water pumping.

5.7 REFERENCES

1. R.K. Singal, '*Non-conventional Energy for Lift Irrigation*', Electrical India, March, 1985'.
2. *Design Criteria for Solar Energy Systems* by R.K. Singal, Electrical India, May, 1986.
3. R.K. Singal, '*Design Proposal for Hot Plate Type Solar Cooker*', Electrical India, July, 1986.
4. R.K. Singal, '*Domestic Solar Refrigerator*', Electrical India, January, 1987.
5. R.K. Singal, '*Development of a Solar Milk Cooler*', Electrical India, November, 1985.

Chapter 6

Hot Plate Type Solar Cooker

6.1 INTRODUCTION

Eighty percent of the basic energy needs of rural India is the provision of cooking energy, which amounts to 0.5 to 1 kWh/person/day with a peak power of 0.2 to 1.2 kW per capita. It is mostly (for 83 percent of rural household) met from traditional fuels like fire-wood, agricultural wastes and cowdung cakes. Cooking with fire-wood and cowdung cakes poses a number of problems for the users and for the society as a whole. The serious implications of deforestation and subsequent soil erosion, pollution and lack of recycling of the natural fertilisers have a significant effect on the overall productivity of these areas. Therefore, it becomes essential to find out an alternate source of cooking fuel.

India is bestowed with abundant supply of solar energy and hence, it can be a very promising source of cooking energy. Large scale solar cooking technology must be attempted to alleviate the demand for cooking fuel. Other non-conventional energy sources such as bio-gas, would be best used to increase the industrial and agricultural productivity of rural areas, while allowing solar energy to provide the bulk of cooking requirements.

Efforts to design and introduce solar cookers have for many years concentrated on two main types: the cooker with a plane collector (box type) and cooker with special parabolic mirrors of average precision. The cost of second type is too high to be used economically in rural areas. The Government of India is trying to introduce box-type solar cookers with financial subsidies but with poor success.

6.2 NON-ACCEPTABILITY OF PRESENT SOLAR COOKERS

Despite Government efforts to introduce box type solar cookers under subsidy programmes, they have failed to find a place in kitchens of the rural household contrary to the expectations. The beneficiaries donot accept solar cookers in daily cooking and their possession has made no impact on their conventional fuel consumption pattern.

6.2.1 Socio-economic Factors

Among the socio-economic factors inhibiting the large scale utilization of solar cookers, initial investment cost is one obstacle to the purchase of solar cooker. Families in rural areas can gather wood and cowdung for fuel for conventional cooking. Furthermore, solar cooking involves alteration in the household routine, since the housewife must prepare the evening meals during day time, well before the traditional time, which increases the additional problem of keeping the food hot. Secondly, the housewife must remain in the hot sun while cooking. On rainy days or when there is insufficient sunshine, conventional fuels have to be used. There is lack of privacy as cooking has to be carried out in the open.

6.2.2 Technical Drawbacks

The technical drawbacks of the present box type solar cooker patronised by the Government may be summarised as follows:

(*i*) The temperatures obtained in the cooking vessel (food) are less than 100°C. It does not ensure hygenic cooking as at some stage of cooking cycle, the temperature of the food must exceed 100°C to kill bacteria.

(*ii*) It takes more time than conventional cooking as it is only a low-temperature, low-energy flux device.

(*iii*) Solar cooking cannot be employed for all modes of cooking processes. For example, chapati making and frying which are very important cooking processes in most part of the country especially north India cannot be carried out in a box type solar cooker. The practice of conventional cooking is very different in India and is a big hinderance to the social acceptability of solar cooking. Solar cooking is very slow and time consuming and some foods have to be pre-cooked before keeping them in the cooker box for final cooking.

(*iv*) There is no provision for storage of heat energy. Cooking has to be carried out while the sun is shining which is an odd time for preparing dinner and breakfast. Also on rainy days and cloudy days when sufficient insolation is not available, auxiliary fuel has to be used.

(*v*) Cooking has to be carried out in the open without privacy and in the sun which is very inconvenient to the housewife. The glare of the mirror glasses can be injurious to the eyes of the housewife and the accompany children.

6.2.3 Study of M.S. University, Baroda

A study was conducted by Dr. (Mrs.) Rachel George, Reader, Home Management Department, Faculty of Home Science, M.S. University, Baroda recently on reasons for non-acceptability of solar cookers and her findings are reported as follows:

(*i*) Lack of Privacy in Cooking : 100 percent

(*ii*) Mirror and glass need special care : 92 percent

(*iii*) Solar cooking should take place during specific periods of the day : 92 percent
(*iv*) Cooking does not get over in time for meals : 75 percent
(*v*) Solar cooking is too time consuming : 72 percent
(*vi*) Solar cooker is too heavy : 72 percent
(*vii*) Food need to be precooked : 50 percent
(*viii*) Cleaning of utensils (blackened from outside) cannot be entrusted to children. : 35 percent
(*ix*) Smell remains in the food and cooker : 25 percent
(*x*) Paint on the cooking containers wears off fast. : 20 percent

The figures indicate the percent response to an opinion poll conducted in rural areas of Gujarat.

The effectiveness of solar cooker can be enhanced by the design of a system which can overcome the above technical and socio-economical problems. The cooker has to be coupled to a heat storage system. It must be capable of storing sufficient heat at a temperature high enough to permit effective cooking later on. It is also desirable to be able to regulate the rate of heat release for cooking.

6.3 DESIGN PROPOSAL

In order to develop a small family size (four persons) solar cooker, a project was undertaken at Regional Engineering College, Kurukshetra. A solar cooker of hot-plate type was designed and successfully constructed. It consists of a flat plate type cooker with mirror boosters. It is coupled to an oil storage insulated tank placed under the cooking platform inside the kitchen through a thermosyphon to the outside collector.

It can provide sufficient flux of heat energy at high enough temperature to a hot plate through a heat pipe. The system would be suitable for cooking of conventional foods at convenient time for breakfast, lunch and dinner inside the kitchen. It would just replace a bottled gas cooking range and would be fitted permanently. It will fit in with the age-old habits and practices of rural households and should be acceptable to the user without reluctance.

6.3.1 Design Data

The following data has been assumed for the design of the cooker after carrying out detailed survey of cooking habits, normalised menu for breakfast, lunch and dinner, cooking times and temperatures for different dishes, energy requirements and burner ratings of bottled gas cooking range. Average sunshine hours and solar radiation are taken for Kurukshetra from the handbooks.

Cooking energy requirements
(4 persons, three meals per day) : 2 kWh/day
Hot Plate Rating : 2 kW.

Cooking Temperature Range	: 150–175°C
Storage Capacity	: 3 kWh.
Annual average solar radiations	: 650 W/m^2.
Annual average sunshine hours/day	: 8 hours.
Annual average wind velocity	: 10 m/s.
Annual average ambient temperature	: 25°C
Design value of latitude	: 30°N.

6.3.2 Component Sizing

Assuming overall efficiency of 15 percent, specific heat of oil as 2.63 kJ/kg-K and oil density at 175°C as 0.905 kg/m^3, the following sizes are worked out;

Total collection area	: 2.5 m^2
Storage volume of hot oil	: 100 litres.

6.4 SYSTEM DESIGN

The basic system design should respond to local climate: sunshine hours, solar radiation level, wind speed, ambient temperature and to energy demand characteristics. The functional flow diagram of the system is shown in Fig. 6.1. It consists of the following sub-systems.

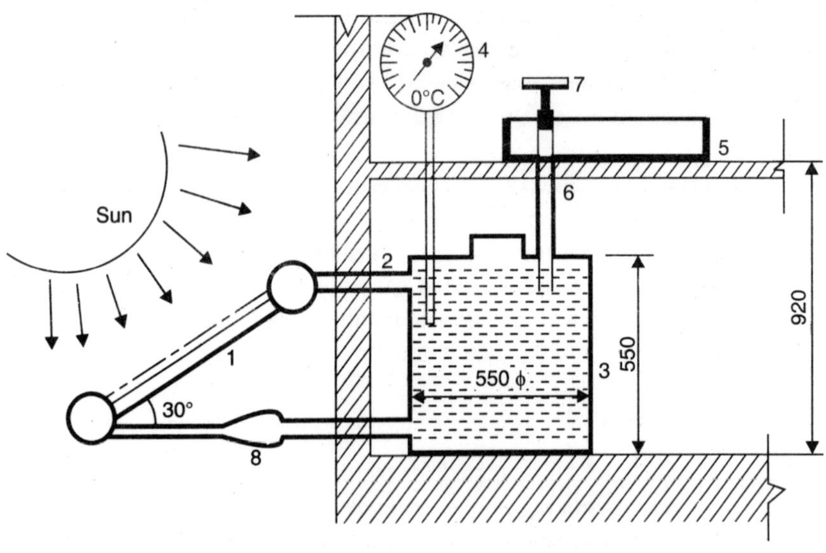

1. Solar collector (1m^2)
2. Thermosyphon (1½″ NB)
3. Hot oil storage tank (100° 1)
4. Thermometer (0–300°C)
5. Hot plate (2 KW)
6. Heat pipe (2 kW)
7. Control valve
8. Non-return valve

Fig. 6.1 Flow diagram of hot-plate-type solar cooker

— Solar collection and conversion.
— Thermal storage.
— Fluid circulation.
— Energy distribution and control.

6.4.1 Solar Collection and Conversion System

The flat plate collectors are easy to fabricate and cheaper than the concentrated type. In addition, flat plate collectors can absorb all the solar insolation, *i.e.*, beam and diffused radiations whereas concentrated type are not sensitive to diffuse radiations. This factor can be very important during cloudy days especially for Indian regions with long monsoon months. The problem of orientation and tracking can be easily handled in flat plate collectors. Concentrating parabolic collectors with special mirros are not considered on economic and above mentioned technical factors.

The technology of flat plate collector is sufficiently developed for other applications such as space heating of small and large buildings, water heating, space cooling, process heat, crop drying, distillation, etc. It will be, therefore, easy to adopt it for solar cooking.

A temperature in the region of 200°C has been obtained in flat plate collector with selective coating of absorber plate and energy reception augmentation with the help of mirror boosters. In order to obtain a temperature of 475 K, we can use augmented flat plates with a concentration ratio of nearly 4 and a|E ratio of 10. Refer to fig. 3 of Author's paper on 'Design Criteria of Solar Energy Systems' published in 15th May Issue of Electrical India.

In order to satisfy the conditions of concentration ratio, four booster plain mirrors are used to get the necessary augmentation. The selective coating can be either chrome black or nickle black with the properties given in Table 6.1.

Table 6.1. Properties of Selective Coatings

Selective Coating	*Shortwave Absorptance, a*	*Longwave Emittance E*	*Ratio a/E*
Black Chrome	0.87	0.09	9.8
Black Nickel Oxide	0.85–0.93	0.06–0.1	14.5–15.5

The arrangement consists of flat plate collector of 1 m^2 surface made from Derco Roll Bond Aluminium panels. Three panels of size 915 mm × 356 mm × 1.5 mm are arranged in parallel and housed in a properly insulated wooden box. The panels are coated with black chrome. Three window glass sheets 3 mm thick and 1000 mm × 1150 mm size are provided as top glazing to cut off losses due to re-radiation and convection from absorber plate. Four plain mirrors of size

1068 m × 915 mm are arranged at the four sides of the panel box with hinges to manipulate necessary tracking of the sun. The collector is installed at 30° (latitude of the site) with the horizontal. The top and bottom mirrors will need only seasonal adjustments whereas side mirrors can be adjusted every hour for optimum collection of solar radiations.

6.4.2 Thermal Storage

Thermal storage is used in most solar systems to provide a thermal capacitance effect. Thermal capacitance is required to damp out the fluctuations of collector energy delivery that occurs in response to short-term fluctuations in sunshine level and diurnal variations related to the 24 hours day-night cycle. In our case, we have to collect solar energy during day time only. On a clear day the energy delivered by the solar system is approximately a sinusoidal function of time with a maximum at noon and minimum near sunrise and sunset. The demand on the thermal storage system will be variable and energy will be extracted three times a day for preparation of breakfast, lunch and dinner. The temperature history of storage for a day will therefore, vary and condition of minimum temperature required for cooking must be met. Also on rainy and cloudy days when sufficient insolation is not available, stored heat should be available for cooking.

The amount of thermal storage is usually subject to economic constraints, since very large storage is generally prohibitively expensive. As a compromise, a storage tank of 100 litres capacity is provided which is equivalent to 3 kWh of heat at 175°C. The hot oil used as working fluid is also the sensible heat storage fluid as it has favourable heat capacity properties.

In order to minimize heat loss and tank material requirements, a right circular cylinder of size 55 cm diameter and 55 cm high fabricated from mild steel of 2 mm thickness has been provided. It can be directly placed on the concrete floor. It is properly insulated with 75 mm thick glass wool sheathed in aluminium sheets. A thermometer of range 0–300°C is provided in the thermowell welded into the storage tank.

6.4.3 Fluid Circulation

The practical use of solar energy requires a means to transport energy from the solar collector to the storage subsystem and in turn to the load or demand points. Any fluid flow is subject to viscous and turbulent resistance to flow that must be overcome by a motive force. The most common motive force is pressure generated by a pump which requires an external source of electrical power.

The natural tendency of a less dense fluid to rise above a more dense fluid can be used to cause fluid motion through a collector. The density difference is created within the solar collector where heat is added to the liquid. This thermosyphon system does not need any pump or electrical power supply.

Since the driving force in a thermosyphon system is only a small density difference and not a pump, larger-than-normal plumbing fixtures must be used to reduce pipe friction losses. We have used $1\frac{1}{2}''$ NB pipes. The flow rate through a thermosyphon system is about 40 litres/m^2 in bright sunshine. After sunset, a thermosyphon system can reverse its flow direction and lose heat to the environment during night. A gravity-type non-return valve is provided in the return cold leg of thermosyphon to avoid reverse circulation of oil. The heat loss from the piping are controlled by proper insulation with asbestos rope.

The working fluid has to be stable at 200°C and should have favourable heat transfer properties. It has to be compatible with aluminium, copper and carbon steel, the materials of construction of solar thermal system. One hundred and ten litres of oil is required for initial fill of the system. Grade Servotherm Medium of Indian Oil Corporation or Hytherm 500 of Bharat Petroleum are suitable oils.

6.4.4 Energy Distribution and Control

The heat pipe is relatively new device for transporting large amounts of heat with a very small temperature drop between heat source and sink. A gravity-assisted heat pipe is used to distribute heat energy from storage tank to a cooking hot plate. The evaporator section of heat pipe is 5 cm long and is inserted vertically from top of storage tank. A condenser length of 10 cm is inserted inside the hot plate. The adiabatic length to suit site conditions is properly insulated with asbestos rope. The heat pipe is made from 32 × 2 mm copper tube of 1 m length. The working fluid is Dowtherm grade E filled at atmospheric pressure after proper evacuation of air. The boiling point of Dowtherm E is 150°C. There are no wicks inside and liquid oil flows down to evaporator section along axial grooves (2 mm × 1 mm deep) cut all along inside of heat pipe.

Much controls and instrumentations are not needed. In addition to a thermometer provided in the oil storage tank, a piston-type valve is provided at the top of heat pipe in the condenser section. The rotation of a small wheel controls the travel of piston in the heat pipe and length of condenser taking part in heat transfer. The heat flow rate from the storage tank through the heat pipe will be proportional to effective condenser length not cut off by piston valve.

The hot plate 200 mm diameter × 125 mm height is made from copper sheet and filled with hot oil for proper heat transfer from heat pipe. It is insulated from all sides except the top cooking surface. The heat pipe has been designed for axial heat flux of 2400 × 10^3 kcal/m^2 and radial heat flux of 1200 × 10^3 kcal/m^2.

The total cost of materials including hot oil charge and fabrication expenses has been ₹ 3000.

6.5 CONCLUSION

The proposed design of hot-plate-type solar cooker overcomes most of the technical and socio-economic drawbacks of the present box-type solar cooker. It fits well with the age-old habits of conventional cooking and should be accepted by the rural population in India without any reservations. It is a permanent fixture comparable in performance to the bottled gas cooking burner in heat flux rates and can provide controlled temperatures required for all types of cooking processes and at suitable timing for preparation of breakfast, lunch and dinner. She can cook in all privacy of her kitchen. It is coupled to a thermal storage system and can last for a day without sunshine. The heat flux rate can be conveniently controlled by turning a small wheel suitably placed at the hot plate. There are no operating and maintenance expenses and life long oil fill is provided.

The prototype cost of ₹ 3000 can be substantially reduced during commercial design and manufacture. With suitable Government subsidies as applicable to other solar devices, this is an ideal design for a low cost solar cooker for adoption in rural and muffasal areas.

6.6 REFERENCES

1. Singal, R.K., '*Design Criteria for Solar Energy Systems*', Electrical India, 15th May, 1986.
2. The Hindustan Times dated 21st October, 1985.
3. R.L. Loftness, '*Energy Handbook*', Van Nostrand Reinhold Company, New York, 1978.
4. A Eggers-Lura, '*Solar Energy in Developing Countries*', Vol. 11, Pergamon Press, Oxford.

Chapter 7

Solar Ahara for Rural Delicacies

The quality of rural life depends upon the availability of cheap and abundant energy for socio-economic activities. Plenty of sunshine available in the village offers an attractive solution to some of the energy problems in rural India. In rural areas, households are the major consumers of energy followed by agriculture and cottage industries. It is mostly met from traditional fuels like wood, dung and agricultural residues. Cooking and domestic heating usually takes place on open fire which has low thermal efficiency of the order of five percent. Cooking with fire-wood and cowdung cakes poses a number of problems for the users and for the society as a whole. The serious implications of deforestration and subsequent soil erosion, pollution and lack of recycling of natural fertilizers have a significant effect on the overall productivity of rural areas. Therefore, it becomes essential to find out an alternative source of domestic fuel. Other non-conventional energy sources such as biogas, wind and micro-hydro, would be best used to increase the industrial and agricultural productivity of rural areas, while allowing solar energy to provide the bulk of energy requirements for cooking and domestic heating.

Efforts to design and introduce solar cookers have for many years concentrated on two main types: the cooker with a plane collector (box type) and cooker with special parabolic mirrors of average precision. The Government of India is trying to introduce box-type solar cookers with financial subsidies but with poor success. This type of cooker has certain technical drawbacks due to very low temperature (less then 90°C) obtained. The cost of second type of solar cookers is too high to be used economically in rural areas. The main reasons are high cost of parabolic mirrors and complicated tracking system required with these types of cookers.

An 'AHARA' is a must for every household in the Indian villages in which a slow fire is maintained for almost whole day with the help of cowdung cakes and firewood. This is a multipurpose cooker-cum-heater with low heat flux inputs. A versatile, multi-purpose, low-cost solar ahara has been developed at Regional Engineering College, Kurukshetra which can be used as a small solar water heater, oil heater, ghee boiler in addition to solar cooker for rural delicacies of India such as rice, dals, sarson-ka-sag, palak and other vegetables and cereals requiring moderate cooking temperatures and low heat flux inputs to preserve taste, flavour and nutritional values of food.

The design of the ahara is based on the use of plane mirrors cut to special shape and size and arranged at suitable angles to approach a paraboloid. The tracking is manually achieved in two axes by the use of simple pipes and joint threads. All the materials have been used so that the same are easily available in the villages and can be assembled locally without the need of any special skills. The total cost of the prototype including materials and manufacturing labour was ₹ 500 only. The cost can be easily reduced further during commercial production. The marketing price of such a heater will be much less than box-type solar cookers patronised by the Government of India. Technically, it is far superior in versatility of applications and a temperature of 125°C is easily obtained for more than four hours on a normal sunny day. The cooking efficiency and cooking time are very favourable as a pressure cooker can also be used with the device. This is not possible in box-type solar cookers.

The solar ahara is a light weight, portable device and can be placed near the south facing wall of the house and tracking can be affected through a window from inside the house. This is a very effective and ideal design for a low-cost solar cooker for adoption in rural and muffasal areas.

Chapter 8

Solar Refrigerator

8.1 INTRODUCTION

Solar energy is better suited to space cooling and refrigeration than to space heating, but until recently this application of solar energy has received little attention. However, energy for air conditioning and refrigeration has been the faster growing segment of the energy consumption due to increasing standard of living and population in India and other developing countries. At the 1975 UNESCO conference on Solar Energy several developing countries stated that small solar driven refrigeration units are urgently needed for preservation of food in rural areas where little electric power is available. Consequently accelerated effort is needed to effect progress in the application of solar energy to space cooling and refrigeration.

The seasonal variations of solar energy are extremely well suited to the space cooling and refrigeration requirements. Since warmest seasons of the year correspond to periods of high incidence of solar energy, it is most available when comfort cooling and refrigeration are most needed. Moreover, the efficiency of solar collector increases with increase in incidence in solar energy and increasing environmental temperature. Consequently, in summer the amount of energy delivered per unit surface area of collector can be larger than that in winter.

Solar cooling and refrigeration are ideally adaptable in India. India is bestowed with high solar insolation and long sunshine hours. Refrigeration units are most needed in rural areas for food preservation where it is difficult to reach with electric power. Therefore, development of small solar-driven refrigeration units is urgently needed for India.

In the light of the above situation, a project was undertaken for the design and development of a small domestic solar refrigerator. The capability of the existing conventional refrigerators was studied and a survey of literature was made to find out a suitable technology for a solar refrigerator to meet the requirements of conventional domestic refrigerator. It was found that a solid absorption-Zeolite refrigerator is most suitable because of absence of moving parts, toxic and corrosive chemicals and expectation of long trouble free operation life. The system is ideally suited to local environment. Heat load and temperature requirements can be met by a convenient and compact sized solar system at competitive price.

There is limited operating experience with solar cooling system. Therefore, the system and components have been designed from the fundamental principles taking into account the operational experience of a conventional refrigeration cycle and special features of the components in a solar system. The project experience can be used to develop small cold storages for preservation of food in rural areas and commercialization of domestic solar refrigerators.

8.2 CONVENTIONAL DOMESTIC REFRIGERATOR

It has been found that the present 165L capacity refrigerator working on vapour compression cycle using Freon-12 as refrigerant is most suitable and popular size in India. The design of the solar domestic refrigerator has therefore, been based on the main specifications of 165L capacity refrigerator. A suitable solar refrigeration system has been sized for fitting onto the cabinet of the present domestic refrigerator of this capacity.

The present conventional refrigerator consists of a well insulated cabinet to maintain a temperature of 8–10°C in the refrigerated space and –4°C in the freezer. The main dimensions of the cabinet are as follows:

Total volume	165L
Food storage capacity	130L
Freezer capacity	35L
Shelf area	0.5 m^2
Door shelf area	0.12 m^2
Insulation	5 cm Polyurethane Foam

An air-cooled extended surface type condenser of sufficient surface area is mounted on the back of the refrigerator. Plate type or wire finned tubular condensers are normally used with 6.35/4.8 mm copper or steel tubes of total length of about 7 m.

The evaporators are housed in the upper space of the cabinet and consists of 7.9/6.35 mm copper tubing of about 5 m length soldered to the plate.

An hermetically sealed compressor of 1/8 hp is spring mounted to isolate vibrations. A filter and capillary tube acts as division point between high pressure and low pressure sides of the cycle and flow of liquid refrigerant is regulated into the evaporator by the capillary tube.

A maximum cooling load of 317 W can be produced by circulation of 125.5 g/min of refrigerant at 1.2 kgf/cm^2 and –25°C in the evaporator and 12.25 kgf/cm^2 and 50°C in the condenser. The maximum coefficient of performance achieved is 4.3.

An experiment was conducted to verify the actual cooling load and temperature obtained in a conventional domestic refrigerator under normal working conditions. A 165L Kelvinator refrigerator was switched off from the power supply and was loaded with usual eatables. The freezer box was filled with 8 kg of ice.

The temperature of the cooled space and amount of ice melted were periodically measured. It was found that similar temperature of 8–10°C was obtained as produced by the refrigerator working on compression cycle. The total ice required for 24 hours operation was 7.5 kg for extreme environmental conditions. In order to take care of a non-sunny day, the solar refrigerator was designed for production of 15 kg of ice by the solar system.

8.3 SELECTION OF SOLAR REFRIGERATION PROCESS

The main requirements of a solar powered domestic refrigerator can be summarized as follows:

1. An ability to keep refrigerated space at 8 to 10°C in an external temperature of + 43°C during day and + 32°C at night. The system should be compact and suitable for attachment to the cabinet of an existing 165L domestic refrigerator.
2. The system should be free of corrosive, toxic and irritating chemicals.
3. The system should have few components, no moving parts, operational simplicity and long trouble-free life.
4. The physical size, weight should be small for case of transportation and installation.
5. It should be possible to manufacture the system and components from local materials and skills.

The following processes can be used for the solar domestic refrigerator:

8.3.1 Photovoltaic-compression System

These systems use the photovoltaic cells which produce electricity when exposed to light. The electricity that is generated is used to charge a battery that operates a 12 or 24 volt d.c. compressor. It provides cooling through an ordinary freon cycle as in conventional domestic refrigerators. Cooling can be provided during period without sun by a store of ice in the refrigerator or by stored surplus power in batteries. The electric power is controlled automatically by a regulator. The system is the most advanced solar cooling technology and many coolers have been marketed as such.

The photovoltaic panels and batteries are very costly, hence initial cost will be very high. Batteries have to be replaced every two to three years making high operating cost. Reliability of photovoltaic panels is unknown at this stage. The major weakness is the complexity and a number of electrical components.

8.3.2 Photovoltaic Thermoelectric Refrigeration System

This method uses the Peltier Effect according to which one end of the element is kept at a high temperature and other at low temperature then emf is produced. In this case electricity is produced using photovoltaic panels exposed to sun. The electricity is used to produce a heat flow through a bimetallic (peltier) solid state element. The cold side of this element is exposed to the inside of the refrigerator and the hot side to outside air. A single element can produce a temperature difference of 27°C between inside and outside faces. The elements can be cascaded together to obtain higher performance. A fan is usually required to remove the accumulated heat from the outside surface. This system has same limitations as photovoltaic compression system.

8.3.3 Ammonia-Water System

Ammonia gas is boiled out of a solution of water and liquid ammonia in a solar collector and is condensed and stored until the collector cools at night and the pressure in the system falls. The liquid ammonia passes into the evaporator and boils at –12°C. The frozen surface of evaporator can make 5 kg of ice in 8 hours. The ammonia gas returns to the collector where it is reabsorbed into a solution with water ready for the next day. The ice can be removed for use or left to cool the refrigerator in times of no sun.

Ammonia has pungent and irritating smell and is not used in conventional domestic refrigerator. It has leakage problem. The complexity of system and welding of pressure parts require special skills. The system development at present is at university level.

8.3.4 Lithium Bromide-Water System

This is a similar system as ammonia-water system with the difference that steam is boiled out of the solution of lithium bromide and water. Steam is condensed and its evaporation at low pressure produces cooling.

In this system the temperature required in the solar collector is in the range of 120°C which cannot be obtained in a flat plate collector. The concentrating type collectors are needed to get the necessary temperature which makes economy unfavourable. It is difficult to obtain adequate circulation especially during regeneration cycle without a pump. The risk exists that liquid lithium bromide will also vaporise.

8.3.5 Calcium Chloride-Ammonia System

Calcium chloride is solid at room temperature and it works as solid absorption system. During day, ammonia gas is driven out of solar collector filled with calcium chloride and cement. The gas is condensed by cooling in a water tank to liquid ammonia and passes into the evaporator. At night as the collector cools and pressure falls, the liquid ammonia passes into the evaporator and boils at –12°C. The frozen surface of evaporator can make 9 kg of ice in 8 hours. The ammonia gas then returns to the collector to be reabsorbed into calcium chloride for the next day. The ice can be removed for use or left to keep the refrigerator cool at times of no sun.

Same objections to the use of ammonia as refrigerant are applicable as were discussed in Water-ammonia system. This system also works at high temperatures of 120°C which cannot be easily obtained in a flat-plate collector. It is difficult to keep solid absorbant as porous and to prevent its clogging.

8.3.6 Solid Absorption Zeolite Refrigeration System

The solar collector is filled with zeolite which is a sandy material available in nature as lava of volcanoes or manufactured as molecular sieve. Water vapour is driven out of the collector by solar heating during the day. The vapours are condensed and stored in a tank until evening. As the collector cools at night due to sky radiation, a vacuum in the system causes the water in the evaporator to boil constantly at a temperature of –2°C at a pressure of 4 mm of Hg. The frozen surface of evaporator can make 9 kg of ice in 8 hours. The water vapours return to the collector for reabsorption into zeolite and the system is ready for the next day. The ice can be removed for use or left to cool the refrigerator at times of no sunshine.

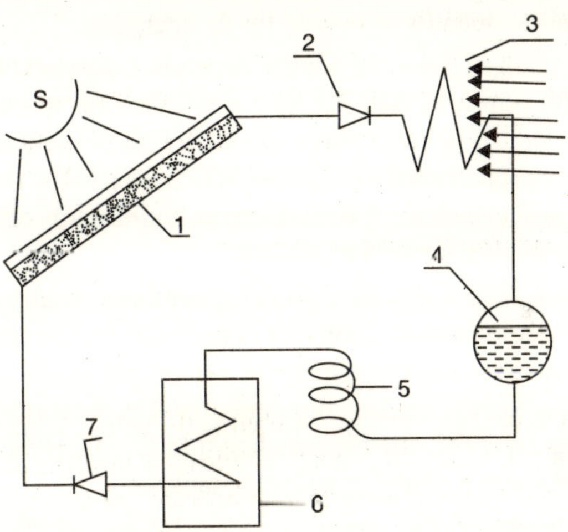

1. 1.5 m^2 Zeolite filled solar collector.
2. 10 NB Non-return valve (Ball type).
3. 4.2 m^2 Panel coil condenser.
4. 20 L Water storage tank.
5. 0.5 mm X 1.4 m Capillary tube.
6. 0.3 m^2 Panel coil evaporator and ice tank.
7. 32 NB Non-return valve (Ball type).

Fig. 8.1 Flow diagram

This system has no moving parts, it is quite compact and has a long operational life. No chemicals are used. Water being the refrigerant, there is no leakage problem. Due to high heat of vaporization of water, the amount of refrigerant circulated is very small as compared to other refrigerants. It can run at collector temperatures of 50°C which are easily obtained in ordinary flat-plate solar collectors. Some manufacturing experience is available in USA for zeolite solar refrigeration.

This system meets most of the requirements for a domestic refrigerator as enumerated above and hence has been selected for the project.

8.4 ZEOLITE

It is possible to use a number of liquid or solid desicants for solar refrigeration. Any material that has high affinity for water vapour can be used. It is regenerated by heating with solar energy. It has been found that zeolites have an unusual absorption property that they can absorb about 30 percent by weight of water at all relative humidities and have been successfully tried in ice-making and solar refrigerators. It is an aluminium-silica complex which has a unique property of absorbing water at low temperatures and giving out a higher temperatures on heating. It can provide refrigeration with excellent engineering efficiency due to their extremely non linear adsorption isothermals. Since, the heat of vaporization of water is largest of any common refrigerant, being ten times larger than that of freons, the zeolite-water vapour combination can provide the most efficient system requiring the smallest quantity of zeolite for its operation.

The adsorption of water in zeolite depends exponentially on at least the second to the fifth power of $\Delta H/RT$, *i.e.*, exp $(\Delta H/RT)^2$ to exp $(\Delta H/RT)^5$. The adsorption of ammonia in water or water vapour in LiBr or in Silica Gel or activated alumina is directly proportional to exp $(\Delta H/RT)$ where ΔH is Heat of Adsorption and T is the absolute temperature. It is this extreme non-linearity of thermal activation that makes zeolite so well suited for cooling.

The zeolite is sealed in an air-tight container that is irradiated by sun. During the day cycle, the zeolite and its container is heated to high temperature. At about 40°C water vapour starts desorbing from the zeolite and partial pressure begins to rise. When the pressure reaches the value determined by the condenser temperature, *i.e.*, 55 mm of Hg for 40°C, the vapours begin to liquify. Heat is rejected to the outside and liquid water is stored in a storage tank.

During night cycle, the zeolite is cooled by sky radiation and is ready to adsorb water vapour even at low pressure. Liquid water absorbs heat from the space to be cooled and is converted into water vapours. If the partial pressure can be maintained at 4 mm of Hg, the water in the evaporator will boil at –2°C. The function of zeolite is to adsorb the water vapour produced by the evaporator maintaining the partial pressure below 4 mm of Hg.

Zeolite system should be free of air. Therefore, the zeolite is placed in hermetically sealed metal panel. The panel is painted black for maximum solar absorption. It is connected through ordinary plumbing to the condenser, water storage tank and evaporator. After the zeolite is charged with water vapour, the whole system is outgassed, evacuated and sealed off.

The zeolite solar panel consists of a flat-plate conventional collector. For the extreme condensation and evaporation pressures of 55 mm and 4 mm of Hg respectively for most zeolites the differential water loading is about 55 percent by weight between ambient temperature and 120°C which is the maximum temperature attainable with flat-plate solar collectors. In most of the practical uses, it is closer to 3 percent by weight. After considerable experimentation and computer analysis, it is found that optimum results are obtained with zeolite capacity of 50 kg/m^2 with a depth of 5 cm. The upper surface of the panel is painted black and pipes are provided at the bottom to permit the water vapours to enter and leave. Each panel has to be leak tested prior to use.

Zeolites can provide refrigeration from the sun without any external power and without any moving parts. The solar refrigerator with an efficiency of 15 percent produces about 900 Wh of cooling per square meter of collector area for a solar input of 6 kWh. This corresponds to about 9 kg. of ice manufactured per day per square metre of collector area.

8.5 SYSTEM DESIGN

The design data for the solar domestic refrigerator has been assumed as follows:

Cooling load	: 15 kg ice
Refrigerant	: Water
Evaporator pressure and temperature	: 4 mm Hg and –2°C
Condenser pressure and temperature	: 55 mm Hg and 40°C
Zeolite absorption capacity for water	: 3% by weight
Average annual solar and sky radiations	: 650 cal/cm^2/day
Average annual sunshine hours	: 250
Average annual day temperature (design)	: + 43°C
Average annual night temperature (design)	: + 32°C
The expected performance of the refrigerator is assumed as follows:	
Total refrigerated volume	: 165L
Evaporator temperature	: –2°C
Refrigerator space temp.	: 8–10°C
Daily ice requirement	: 7.5 kg
Total design capacity	: 15 kg ice (1350 kcal)
Storage capacity	: Two days of bad weather.
Heating per day at 55°C @ 15% collector efficiency	: 1460 kcal.
Cooling by sky radiations at 32°C	: 1460 kcal.
Daily average C.O.P.	: 1350/1460 = 0.92
Total cost of one unit	: ₹ 4500

8.6 SPECIFICATIONS

The main specifications of the solar refrigerator are worked out as follows:

1. Collector

Collector type	:	Flat Plate
Collector area	:	1.5 m^2
Dimensions	:	0.75 × 2.0 m
Absorber panel material	:	All copper, 0.5 mm thick.
Surface treatment	:	Copper black on copper.
Glazing	:	Double 3 mm low iron glass.
Case material	:	Aluminium extrusions 2.15 m × 0.9 m × 0.15 m
Insulation back, edge	:	Glass wool 50 mm thick
Sealants and gaskets	:	Rubber
Manifold details	:	Outlet 10 NB Copper tube Inlet 32 NB Copper tube
Weight	:	100 kg.
Method of installation	:	Wall mounted at an angle of latitude of the site.

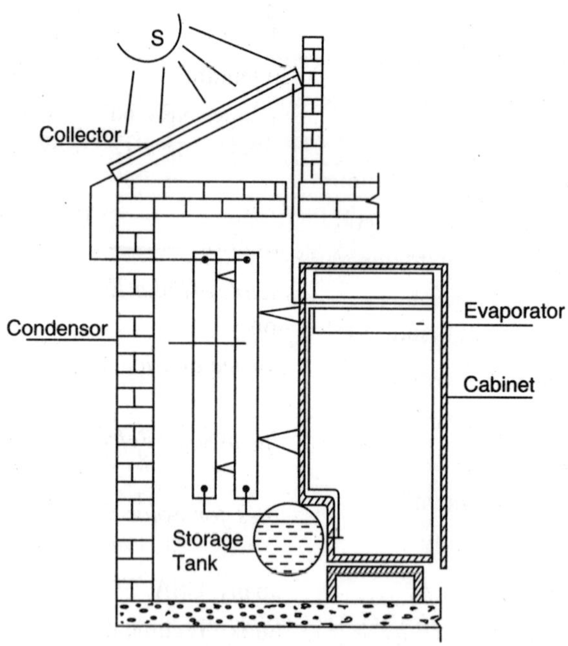

Fig. 8.2 Arrangement drawing

2. Evaporator

Daily refrigeration effect	:	1350, kcal.
Design heat rate	:	1350/8 = 168.75 kcal/hr.

Heat transfer coefficient	:	342 kcal/hr-m^2–°C (water to water)
Temperature terminal	:	2°C
Heat transfer area	:	0.247 m^2
Type	:	Panel coil, double embossed P type evaporator immersed in water.
Size	:	30 cm × 30 cm.

3. Condenser

Refrigerant flow rate	:	0.251 kg/hr.
Heat rate of rejection	:	168.25 kcal/hr.
Heat transfer coefficient from steam to air	:	8.52 W/m^2 –°C
Temperature terminal	:	5°C
Heat transfer area	:	3.95 m^2
Panel size	:	75 cm × 115 cm. Two nos.

4. Capillary Tube.

Material	:	Copper
Size	:	1.5/0.5 mm × 1.47 m length.

5. Miscellaneous

Water Storage tank	:	MS tank 20L capacity. 50 cm diameter × 25 cm length.
Low pressure piping	:	32 NB copper NRV ball type 4 cm LDPE
High pressure piping	:	10 NB copper NRV 1-5 cm aluminium.

8.7 REFERENCES

1. Frank Kreith and J.F. Kreider, '*Principle of Solar Engineering*', Hemisphere Publishing Corporation, Washington.
2. *Solar Refrigerators for Vaccine storage and Ice Making*, Selected Article from ASSET, Vol. 6, No. 1, 1984.
3. Tchernev, D.I. '*Use of Natural Zeolite in Solar Refrigeration*' ASSET, Vol. 6, No. 5, 1984.
4. Tchernev, D.I., '*The Use of Zeolites for Solar Cooling*', The Zeopower Company, USA.
5. Trade literature of Zeopower Company, USA.
6. Panel Coil Heat Transfer Handbook, Technical data No. 358 A, Dean Products, New York.
7. ASHARE Handbook — System and Equipment.
8. Trade literature of Kelvinator India Ltd.

Chapter 9

Solar Milk Cooler

9.1 INTRODUCTION

India is essentially an agricultural country with 78 percent of its population living in rural villages. Population-wise the distribution of villages is as follows:

Population			*No. of Villages*	*Per cent of Total*
Up to		499	349995	62.0
500	to	999	118602	21.0
1000	to	1999	65101	11.6
2000	to	4999	26400	4.6
5000	to	9999	3404	0.6
10000	and	above	774	0.2
	Total		564276	100.0

About 95 percent of the total are small villages with population less than 2000. On an average, the cattle population is 50 percent of human population in Indian villages. The total milk production per village per day on an average may be taken as 2000 liters; out of which the milk producers consume 25 percent for self use and convert about 45 percent into milk products like ghee, paneer and khoa. Therefore, 500–600 litres of milk per village is available for sale as liquid milk per day.

Normally, at present this milk is sold as such and its chilling is done by the agencies procuring it. A village level chilling/cooling facility will surely be advantageous as it will make possible collection of evening milk also once in a day which is more economical than twice a day collection requiring use of available collection, transport and chilling facilities twice each time operating much below their rated capacities. There will thus be large savings through once-a-day collection. For example reduction in route kilometerage only can result in savings of about 12.5 percent of the procurement cost.

Rural processing of milk can add value to the product and increase rural income. The fluid milk can be cooled to the prescribed temperatures by the producers or their co-operatives and keep the milk fresh till the time it is boiled by the consumers for use. Pasteurisation of milk is not necessary as consumers even otherwise boil the pasteurised milk and wastage of energy for double heating can be avoided.

At present, some manufacturers have developed milk cooling and storing cabinets suitable for rural areas. Typical specifications of such chillers produced by Larsen & Toubro are given below:

Capacity (Litres)	*Connected Load (kW)*	*Budgeted price (₹ in Lacs)*
500	2.5	1.32
1000	3.7	2.50
2000	5.0	3.00

The milk is quickly cooled from ambient temperature to below critical temperature and further cooled and stored at 4°C. The cooling is achieved by mechanical refrigeration and therefore, electricity is required for its operation. Unfortunately electrical power is not available in most of the villages and rural electrification is very expensive and practically difficult in far flung areas in a vast country of India's size. On the other hand, India is bestowed with plenty of sunshine all the year round, and development of a suitable solar milk cooler to meet the above requirements of cooling and storage of fresh milk can be a boon to the rural economy and white revolution. Few components, no moving parts, operational simplicity, long repair free life are essential requisites of a good design of a milk cooler for rural adoption.

9.2 SOLID ABSORPTION-ZEOLITE REFRIGERATION: BASIC OPERATING CYCLE

Zeolite is a mineral found in many parts of the world and has special adsorption properties. It can adsorb water vapour, ammonia, carbon oxides and freons, all with 30 percent by weight. The zeolite-water vapour combination is the most efficient system as it requires minimum amount of zeolite due to largest heat of vaporisation of water. The adsorption of water in zeolite is a function of temperature and pressure and nonlinear dependence on pressure makes zeolite very favourable for solar applications.

The zeolite is sealed in an air-tight container irradiated by the sun. During the day cycle, the zeolite is heated to a temperature of about 120°C. At about 40°C, water vapour starts desorbing from the zeolite, and its partial pressure rises. At condensing temperature of 40°C, the partial pressure is about 55 mm Hg and vapour begins to liquify as heat is rejected to the environment. The liquid water is stored in a tank. During the night cycle, the zeolite is cooled by convection to ambient temperature and sky radiation.

Liquid water from the storage tank is introduced into the evaporator, where it absorbs heat from the space to be cooled and is converted into water vapour. If partial pressure is 5 mm Hg, the water in the evaporator boils at –2°C. The zeolite adsorbs the water vapour produced by the evaporator and a partial pressure is maintained below 5 mm Hg. The heat of adsorption is rejected to the atmosphere. The zeolite is fully loaded corresponding to the partial pressure and is ready for next day cycle.

$$Na_2\,Al_2\,SiO_2 + \times \cdot H_2O = Na_2\,Al_2\,SiO_2 \cdot \times\, H_2O$$

The above cycle can be utilized for the development of zeolite solar cooler.

9.3 ZEOLITE SOLAR COOLER

Zeolite solar cooler can be used to produce cooling effect and manufacture ice using sun's rays without any external power and without moving parts. A solar cooler having an efficiency of 15 percent can produce about 0.9 kWh of cooling for each square meter of collector area receiving a solar input of 6 kWh. This amount of cooling corresponds to about 9 kg of ice manufactured per day for each square meter of collector. This principle can be used to produce ice, refrigerators to store vaccine, domestic refrigerators, on-side refrigeration of perishable produce and tropical fruits, in-the-field refrigeration of high-cost perishable products etc. Its major applications can be in developing countries like India where energy costs are high and electricity unavailable, unreliable and expensive. It can be of great importance to the fishing industry, especially for refrigeration of fresh fish and other seafood in the remote fishing villages in tropical countries. However, it has a great potential for dairy farmers and rural milk producers.

9.4 MILK COOLER DESIGN

Possible design of a solar milk cooler can be as per the following specifications:

9.4.1 Solar Panel

The zeolite solar panel resembles a conventional flat-plate collector. After the zeolite is charged, the whole system is outgassed, evacuated and hermetically sealed. The panels have a zeolite capacity of about 50 kg/m^2 and requires a depth of 50 mm. The upper surface of the panel is painted black for maximum solar absorption. The water loading is 5 to 7 percent by weight of zeolite for a temperature range of 40°C to 120°C. The inlet and outlet pipes are connected at the bottom of the panel to permit water vapour to enter and leave. The panel is leak-tested prior to use.

The system is ideally suited to local manufacture, but the zeolite will have to be imported and skill is required to prepare zeolite — filled collector and evacuate the system. In order to avoid the import of zeolites, synthetic zeolites can be tried.

It may be interesting to try strong Acid Cation Exchange resins in either Na or K form as desicants in place of natural zeolites, which are indigenously manufactured.

9.4.2 Condenser

The air-cooled condenser fin-pipes can be fixed at the back of sloping panels. The condenser pressure will be 55 mm Hg corresponding to ambient air temperature of 40°C. The condensed vapours during the desorption cycle run by gravity into the flooded evaporator.

9.4.3 Cooling-cum-Storing Tank

The cooling-cum-storing tank can be made from single-embossed panel coils of stainless steel, the inside being plain sheet and outside made of embossed sheet. This design establishes thermosyphon circulation in the walls during the cooling cycle. The design acts as a very efficient heat exchanger thus reducing the temperature difference between milk and water vapour to less than 0.5°C. As water storage is in the bottom, it makes possible to cool even small quantities of milk. At a pressure of 5 mm Hg, water will boil at –2°C in the evaporator coils and this low pressure is maintained due to adsorption of water vapour by zeolites.

The walls and roof of the tank are covered with 150 mm thick polyurethane insulation having a loss coefficient of 0.2 W/m^2. °C.

Unlike conventional milk coolers using freons or ammonia as refrigerant and brine as secondary fluid, solar milk cooler works with only one fluid. As there are no moving parts or corrosive chemicals and there is no reduction in the adsorption ability of zeolite, it is estimated, the system would work for more than ten years.

9.4.4 Auxiliary Heat

The cooler uses only solar energy and can be used in rural areas where electricity is unavailable, unreliable or expensive. The collector panel can be provided with pipes that run through the zeolite panel to provide auxiliary heat whenever the sun is not shining. The farmer could then start a small fire from straw, cowdung or other local fuels and let the hot gases from the fire pass through the pipes in the zeolite panel, thereby heating the zeolite and causing desorption.

9.5 REFERENCES

1. D.I. Tchernev, '*Use of Natural Zeolites in Solar Refrigeration*', ASSET, Vol. 6, No. 5, 1984, Tokyo.
2. '*Solar Refrigeration for Vaccine Storage and Ice Making*', ASSET, Tokyo, Vol. 6, No. 1, 1984.
3. D.O. No. DS|84-85|4|731 dated 24th May, 1984 from Dairy Superintendent, National Dairy Research Institute, Karnal.

Part 4
Hydro Energy

Chapter

10

An Alpine Hydro Village

10.1 INTRODUCTION

India is a country of villages. These villages vary in size and population and are scattered all over the country. Some of these are located on the hills and in dense forests and can be reached only on foot or by pony. They have no road connections to other villages, towns and cities. The population of these villages may be one hundred to two hundred people. Most of them earn their living by cultivating the land, growing fruits and some of them may be craftsmen who earn their living by weaving woollen carpets, by making earthen pots, by weaving baskets and even by making beautiful carved articles from wood, brass of other local materials. Some of them keep cattles like cows, sheep and goats and make their living on animal yields. In a nutshell, life is hard and hilly villages are vary low income areas.

The main wealth of hilly areas is vegetation varying according to temperature, soil and rain and mainly depends upon the altitude. Near the base of the mountains the vegetation will be thick evergreen forests while the top of the mountains will have no vegetation, but will be covered with eternal snows. The vegetation belts of the Himalayas are given in Table 10.1.

Table 10.1. Vegetation Belts of the Himalayas

Altitute (m)	*Description*	*Trees*	*Fruits*	*Crops*
0-750	Tarai	Sal, Bamboo	Tropical Fruits	Barley, Rice, Tea, Potatoes
750-1000	Deciduous Forests	Oak, Horse-chestnut	Temperate Fruits	Rice
1000-1600	Mixed Forests	Oak, Beech	Walnuts	Tea
1600-3300	Coniferous Forest	Pine, Chir, Fir, Deoder, Cedar, Spruce	—	—
3300	Timber	Line		
3300-4200	Alpine Grasslands	—	—	—
4200	Snow	Line		
4200-8500	Eternal Snow	—	—	—

The valleys are surrounded by the mountains and are protected from the cold winds blowing on the mountains. The climate is warm and the soil is more fertile than that of the mountains. In almost all valleys, there are rivers and sometime lakes. Good crops especially fruits like apples, pears, cherries, etc., can be grown in the valleys.

India has made great strides in industrialisation during post independence years. This has brought prosperity to a selected few and created concentrated centres of employment near the industrial complexes and big cities where economic activities have flourished. The material and energy resources have been diverted to feed these industrial and commercial 'gluttons'. The high technology industry could not penetrate the hilly areas. The population of these areas felt neglected and many of them are flocking to the new economy centres in search of their livelihood. The continuous migration of population and uneven distribution of wealth, material and energy resources have created many social and political problems which can lead to very serious consequences, if not further checked.

10.2 NEED FOR CHANGE

The continuous flux of population to new economy centres has created the problems of mushrooming of slums and destruction of social life; the introduction of high technology will give birth to widespread unemployment. These problems can explode with very serious consequences. These can be checked only by adoption of Gandhian model of socio-economic development with village as the unit. Each unit must be self-sufficient economically and the ratio of exports to imports of goods into a village must be more or equal to one. The development, welfare and prosperity of hilly village depend upon the availability of cheap and abundant energy for domestic cooking, heating and lighting, community development, irrigation water, mechanised agriculture and small industrial parks based on local materials.

Transportation of commercial fuels like coal, diesel and petrol over long distances to hilly areas is very difficult and transmission and distribution of electricity through power grids to far flung areas are prohibitively expensive. The farmers and, craftsmen are not in a position to pay for high costs of energy, thus small scale industries in these areas are reduced and there are limited irrigation possibilities in agriculture.

10.3 APPROPRIATE TECHNOLOGY

The modern high technologies donot adopt to rural ecology. Only appropriate technology involving local resources, manpower and raw materials can ensure environmental harmony and sustainability of the development. However, there should be provision for upgrading of technology in the future. The wealth of the hills can be increased by inputting ample energy and technology to increase agricultural, forest and animal yields. Appropriate technology can be worked out by a technical institute specially established for the development of hilly areas. An energy production technique based on local resources and appropriate technology which can be taken care by trained local people for its design, manufacture, installation, operation and maintenance is ideally suited. The utilisation of energy flowing water through small hydel schemes is a good example of appropriate technology for the development of hilly areas. An alpine hydro village should meet most of its energy requirements from small hydel schemes. One such model is described in the following paragraphs.

The utilisation of hydroenergy to operate agricultural and industrial devices is one of the oldest and widespread techniques of human achievements. Hydraulic rams have been used to raise water for lift irrigation and drinking purposes. Water mills of various types have been used to generate mechanical power to drive irrigation pumps, machine tools and small electric generators. The Himalaya Mill is well known in the mountain areas from Afganistan to Burma which is mostly used for grinding grains. The present model of alpine hydro village is based on these devices and are briefly described before discussing the hydro model proper.

10.4 HYDRAULIC RAM

Hydraulic ram is a contrivance to raise a part of large amount of water available at some height, to a greater height. This can be employed in hilly areas where some natural source of water like a spring or a stream is available at some altitude. Work done by a large quantity of water in falling through a small height is used to raise a small part of it to a greater height. Action of water hammer makes it feasible.

No external power is, therefore, required to work this machine. Other attractions are: negligible amount of maintenance and supervision costs, continuous operation, high efficiency, quiet operation and possibility of automatic adjustment of water supply. The liftable volume of water diminishes asymptotically with lifting height. In case of medium lifting heights the hydraulic ram operates with an efficiency absolutely comparable to a piston pump of the same performance.

As the hydraulic ram does not need a driving unit, it is to be considered as ideal for lift irrigation and supply of drinking water for hilly areas, where the supply in fossil energy carriers or electricity is problematic. The hydraulic ram operates with water streams of 1 to 40 m^3/s and fall heads of 1.5 to 30 m and with lifting heights up to 300 m. These are a number of different types which can be distinguished by the operation of oscillating valves.

Hydraulic ram is a simple and rugged device for operating irrigation schemes. This can be easily assembled from local materials. The proposed technical institute for the development of hilly areas has to put in some development work to improve the performance and adoption of hydraulic ram to irrigation.

10.5 HIMALAYA MILL

It is a vertical shaft, horizontal runner hydraulic turbine used to drive grain mills. The wooden radial blades are attached to a boss fitted into a wooden or steel shaft. The water is fed through open wooden channel. It produces about 0.5 hp with a water head of 1 m. There are about 10000 such mills scattered in the hilly areas from Afganistan to Burma producing power equivalent of about 45000 kWh daily.

The horizontal water wheel can be improved in performance to raise its efficiency substantially so that it can be adopted in a small-scale industry park as a prime-mover for flour mills, thrashers, rice-husking machines, vertical lathe, circular saw, triphammer, small electrical generator, carpet loom etc. The vertical lathe can be used by the craftsmen to produce wooden vessels and trip hammers for embossed copper vessels. The saw mill can be used by the carpenters. All these machines can be employed together to meet the local needs to produce domestic and agricultural implements and packing boxes for the export of fruits and other products.

The himalaya mill can be developed into an efficient and modern Pelton turbine using metallic buckets fitted to a vertical shaft supported on roller bearings. The water can be directed onto the buckets, through adjustable nozzle from a piping system collecting water from natural streams existing abundantly in the hilly areas. The stopping of turbine can be achieved through manual brakes and load/speed regulation by the nozzle. The design documentation can be provided by the proposed technical institute for the development of hilly areas and machine can be manufactured in the small scale industry park. The output of the machines can be standardised at 5 to 10 kW.

The tail race water can be recirculated by lifting it with a hydraulic ram for irrigation purposes.

10.6 FLOATING MILL

Poncelet water wheel or a Darrius Turbine rotor can be submerged in a river or water stream available in the hilly areas to tap current energy from water of high speeds. The mechanical energy thus obtained is used for driving irrigation pumps, small electric generators and small compressors for cold storages and ice mills. The small cold storages are necessary in the hilly areas to store potatoes and other perishable goods to get better returns. Ice mill can be used to chill and store milk before it is sent to bigger collection centres.

The electricity generated is required to light the houses, schools, community centres and to run TV sets and other domestic devices. All these measures can improve the wealth of the village multifold and raise the standard of living of the population which will arrest their migration to big cities.

The blades of the water mills can be made from fabricated steel, ferrocement, glass fibre or timber depending upon the availability of the local materials and skills. The power output depends upon the swept area and cube of water velocity and very large energy can be tapped from hill streams flowing at high speeds.

The turbine rotor can be mounted on a pontoon or may be hung from a bridge or a beam over the stream. The pontoon can float on two rows of barges or empty oil drums under which wooden keels are fixed. The mooring cable can be adjusted with a winch to ensure sufficient angle of the keels to the current direction so that water side thrust on the keel keeps the pontoon at a distance from the bank. A turbine with swept area of 4 m^2 and rotor efficiency of 25 percent can give an output of 8 kW at a water current speed of only 2 m/s. These turbines can be adopted to run small cold storages and ice mills, irrigation pumps and to produce all the electricity requirements of the village.

10.7 HYDRO VILLAGE

A typical layout of an alpine hydro village is shown in Fig 10.1. The capacity and number of each type of hydro machines will depend upon the size of the village and characteristics of available water stream. The following units have been included in the scheme.

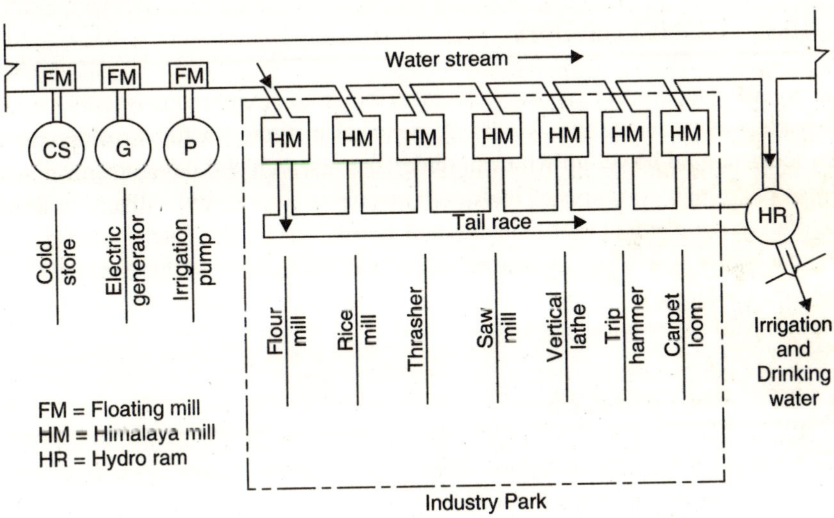

Fig. 10.1. Hydro village

1. A small cold storage and ice mill run by a floating water mill. The capacity of the plant can be around 10 kW. Such cold storages can be built along the flow of water stream to store potatoes, fruits and other perishable products. This will help to avoid spoilage of such products and realize better returns by disposing off uniformly over the year. Similarly the ice mills attached to the coil storage can be used to chill and store the milk cooperatively and can be drawn for disposal to collection centres and self use efficiently.
2. Electrical generator run by a floating water mill. The capacity will match the village requirement of electricity for lighting, heating, cooking and

running of radios, TV sets and other small electrical gadgets in the houses, schools, dispensaries and community centres.

3. Irrigation pump run by a floating water mill. The capacity will suit the irrigation water requirements.
4. Industry Park consisting of flour mills, rice mills, thrashers, saw mills, vertical lathes, trip hammers, carpet looms, etc., run by improved Himalaya mills individually. The capacities can be standardised at 5 to 10 kW each. The industry park will meet all the domestic and agricultural requirements and make the village independent of imports of implements and spare parts. This will help to produce the crafts goods like wooden, brass and other vessels, toys, beauty carvings, woollen carpets for exports with mechanical aids. All packing boxes for export of forest, agricultural and animal yields will be prepared in the industry park.
5. Hydraulic ram to lift the used water from tail race for irrigation and domestic water consumption.

10.8 CONCLUSIONS

The proposed alpine hydro village can meet the productivity requirements for self-sufficiency as per Gandhian Model. A technical institute for the development of hilly areas should be set up who can undertake research and development for the improvement and adoption of hydraulic machines for a hydro village. It should also plan and implement such schemes and monitor the results. Such hydro villages can go a long way in bringing prosperity and self-sufficiency to these villages. The population migration can be arrested and country can be prepared to absorb high technology in the required sectors.

10.9 REFERENCES

1. Singal, R.K., '*Floating Type Micro Hydro Power Plants*', Electrical India, Bombay, 30th September 1984.
2. Singal, R.K., '*Non-Conventional Energy for Lift Irrigation*', Electrical India, Bombay, March, 1985.
3. '*Upgrading and Further Development of Traditional Devices for the Utilisation of Hydro Energy*', Bremen Overseas Research and Development Association, Bremen.

Chapter 11

Floating Type Micro Hydro Power Plants

11.1 INTRODUCTION

India has made great strides in industrialisation during post independence years. This has brought prosperity to a selected few and created concentrated centres of employment near the industrial complexes and big cities where economic activities have flourished. The material and energy resources have been diverted to feed these industrial and commercial 'gluttons'. The high technology industry could not penetrate the traditionally agricultural rural remote areas where nearly 78 percent of India's population live. The rural population felt neglected and many of them are flocking to the new economy centres in search of their livelihood. The continuous migration of population and uneven distribution of wealth, material and energy resources have created many social and political problems which can lead to very serious consequences, if not further checked.

The solution of the problem lies in concerted efforts for the development, welfare and prosperity of the rural areas which in turn depend upon the availability of cheap and abundant energy for domestic cooking, heating and lighting, community development, irrigation water, mechanised agriculture and small industries.

Transportation of commercial fuels like coal, diesel and petrol over long distances to remote and rural areas is very difficult and transmission and distribution of electricity through power grid to far flung areas are prohibitively expensive. The farmers and craftsmen are not in a position to pay for high costs of energy, thus small scale industries in these areas are reduced and there are limited irrigation possibilities in agriculture.

The modern high technologies do not adopt to rural ecology. An energy production technique based on renewable source and appropriate technology which can be taken care by trained local people for its operation and maintenance problems is ideally suited. Only appropriate technology involving local resources, manpower and raw materials and environment can ensure environmental harmony and sustainability of the development. The utilisation of energy in flowing water through micro hydro schemes is a good example of appropriate technology for rural development.

11.2 SMALL HYDEL PROJECTS IN INDIA

Hydropower, available free of cost in the form of flowing water, is an important, pollution free, renewable source of energy. The large potential of hydroenergy available from flowing water in the rivers and irrigation canals, however, still remains untapped, since generating power on a small scale from low and ultra low head drops of 3 to 20 metres has not been an economic proposition because of the high civil and equipment costs as well as high operating cost to be incurred per unit of power generated. The situation is further deteriorated by very low load factors in rural areas.

China has developed 1200 MW of power by small hydel projects by creating water heads of about 5 m along the rivers. It is estimated that 5000 MW capacity of power can be created in India with the help of small hydro turbines of 200 kW to 1000 kW capacity each. M/s. Jyoti Limited, Baroda have the necessary know-how and capacity to manufacture these small hydro turbines, see Table 11.1. There are also other organisations showing interest in the manufacture of such small sets. Bharat Heavy Electricals Ltd. also has the necessary know-how which can be passed on to some ancillary unit for quick manufacture of small hydro turbine without disturbing their main manufacturing plan for large sets.

Table 11.1. Manufacturing Range of Jyoti Ltd. for Small Hydel Sets

Type of turbine	*Operating head range (m)*	*Output range (kW)*
Pelton	100 to 400	50 to 6000
Turgo Impulse	50 to 200	25 to 3000
Francis	20 to 200	50 to 3000
Propeller/Kaplan	2 to 30	10 to 6000
Horizontal Tubular	2 to 25	10 to 6000

Due to civil costs of dams, water conduits and diversion channels, independent small hydel projects become very costly. It may cost ₹ 18000 per kW installed. Such projects should be planned on the basis of multiple purpose use of water resources such as irrigation and power generation. Even though these schemes are costlier when compared with the cost of unit power generation from major hydel projects, these are encouraging keeping long-term energy availability in view. Also hydropower is renewable in nature, once built, there is built-in protection against inflation of cost, water is available essentially free, it can be instantaneously switched on, it need not run continuously.

According to the size of hydroturbine, the small hydel projects may be classified as:

Micro Hydel Projects : 50 to 100 kW
Mini Hydel Projects : 100 to 1000 kW
Small Hydel Projects : 2 MW to 15 MW.

Small hydel projects can be completed in four to five years, mini and micro projects in three years provided civil works of irrigation projects are already completed. Here water released for irrigation only is used and power is therefore, generated for 6 to 7 months a year.

In Maharashtra, 130 schemes of various categories of small hydro projects of about 1100 kW capacity for a layout of ₹ 2000 millions have been planned. A separate circle has been created in UK State Electricity Board with headquarters at Nainital for small hydel projects. Sixteen micro hydel schemes are already functioning in eight hill districts of UK with total installed capacity of 7730 kW. Four schemes are under construction for a total cost ₹ 3.37 crores. The total installed capacity after completion of these schemes will be 8830 kW. Other 32 schemes of 20000 kW are in the pipeline.

Other hilly states are also going for small and micro hydel schemes in a big way.

11.3 RIVER CURRENT ENERGY

Western Ghats of Maharashtra and regions of Uttra Khand, Himachal Pradesh, Jammu & Kashmir, Sikkim and North Eastern States located in the Himalayas are suitable sites for small hydel projects where medium to high heads can be available. Equipment costs are low in the high head schemes. As we come down the hills, the available head decreases and equipment costs go up. For example, the cost of one

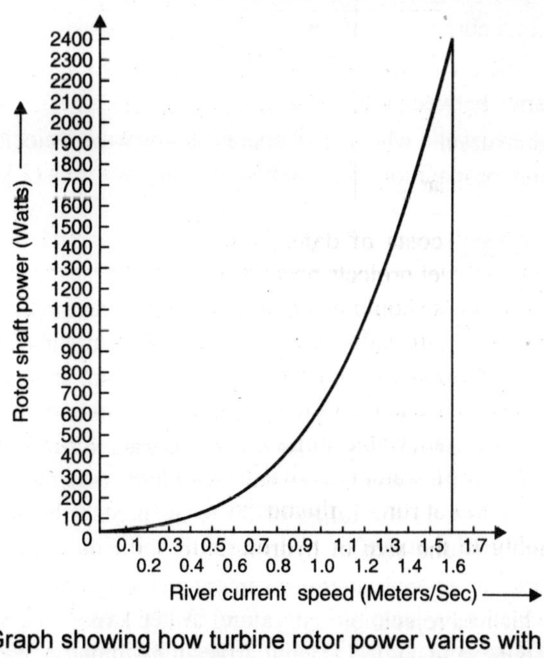

Fig. 11.1. Graph showing how turbine rotor power varies with river current speed for a turbine with swept areas 4 m^2 and rotor efficiency 25%

hydro set of horizontal tubular design of 3.2 kW capacity operating at a head of 3 m may be ₹ 1.28 lacs, *i.e.*, ₹ 40000 per kW installed. The civil costs are site-specific but taking 30 percent of equipment cost, the total installed cost will be a high value of ₹ 52000 per kW installed.

Most of our rivers flow through flat terrains which can be harnessed to produce power much in excess of 5000 MW as estimated above. Chinese model is difficult to develop due to different topography in India. Special 'zero' head turbines operating on kinetic energy of flowing water should be developed to harness huge river current energy. The civil costs of micro hydel power projects can be drastically cut by using floating type plants. There is no need of diversion channels, deep excavation and massive foundations. The floating plant consists of two floats with a vertical (or horizontal) runner in between, which rotates by the velocity of water. The capacity developed is a function of the size of the runner and cube of water current speed. The rotational speed of runner is rather low and electric generator can be operated via a transmission gear. The floating plant moves up and down with water level and gives constant performance all the year round which is a big advantage over firmly installed water turbines especially during monsoons.

The current energy of flowing water which can be exploited by floating type power plant may be expressed as:

$$P = 1/2\, A\, V^3 E \text{ (kW)}$$

where P = Power generated

A = Embrassing area of runner (m^2)

V = Water current speed (m/s)

E = Efficiency of runner and depends upon the type of the runner and varies between 0.5 to 0.85.

Although hydraulic wheels will operate at low water velocities, it is unlikely to be an economic proposition in current speeds below 1 m/s (2 knots).

11.4 PONCELET WATER WHEEL

In ancient times, floating mills were used in Germany on large rivers such as the Rhine, the Weser and the Elbe to drive electric generators and machine tools. A vertical undershot water wheel consisting of a horizontal shaft and radial blades fixed to it, was fitted on the side of a barge which was either moored to the bank or firmly anchored in the stream. A smaller barge was used to support the other end of the shaft. The hulls of the barges were built with local materials. The efficiencies realised were very low, in the range of 20 to 30 percent because of bad blade geometry (straight radial blades).

Poncelet water wheel is an improvement on the straight blades of undershot water wheel, which have suitable curvature. Water strikes the vanes practically without shock (inlet vane angle 15°) and drives it by impulse. Water is discharged from the blades almost vertically downwards. The efficiencies achieved are 55 to 65 percent.

The main drawback of such machines is low power output for a given size and weight because at any instant only a small part of it is actually in the water being driven by the current while the rest of the machine is idle.

11.5 DARRIEUS TURBINE ROTOR

Darrieus turbine rotor is similar to modern vertical-axis wind turbine which was first introduced in France by G.J.M. Darrieus in 1920's. Its configuration consists of four hydrofoil blades which rotate at much higher speed than the water current speed. The speed of rotation is primarily dependent upon the machine overall dimensions. It has relatively low starting torque. Because of simplicity of the blade design and because they are relatively thin, blade fabrication costs are low. They require no pitch control for synchronous applications.

Two prototypes have been developed by Intermediate Technology. Development Group, London and are shown in Fig. 11.2 and 11.3. The blades can be made out of timber or fabricated from steel, ferrocement or glass fibre. The expected performance from these models are plotted in Fig. 11.1.

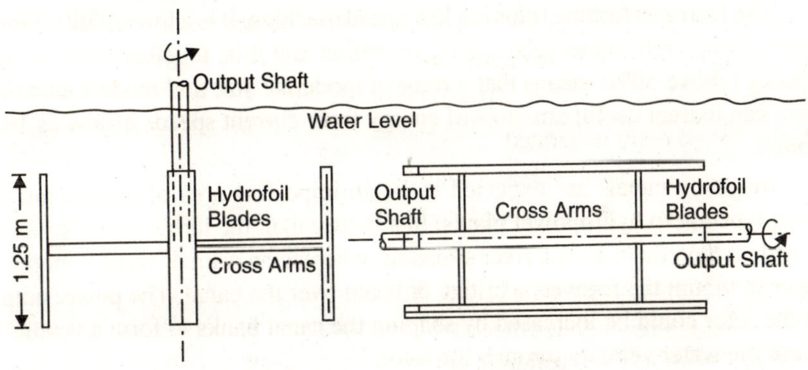

Fig. 11.2. Vertical axis rotor 13.5 R.P.M. in 1 m/s current power take off above surface swept area 3.75 m²

Fig. 11.3. Horizontal axis rotor 32 R.P.M. in 1 m/s current power take offs under water swept area 3.75 m²

11.6 INSTALLATION

Floating type micro hydropower plants are suitable for use in situations where there is no 'head' of water available and is designed to extract kinetic energy from a river or canal current. Therefore, appropriate sites are along the banks of large rivers or on irrigation canals.

As the energy flux depends upon the cube of water velocity, the latter must be as large as possible. The depth of water required for a 4 m^2 runner is atleast 2.5 m.

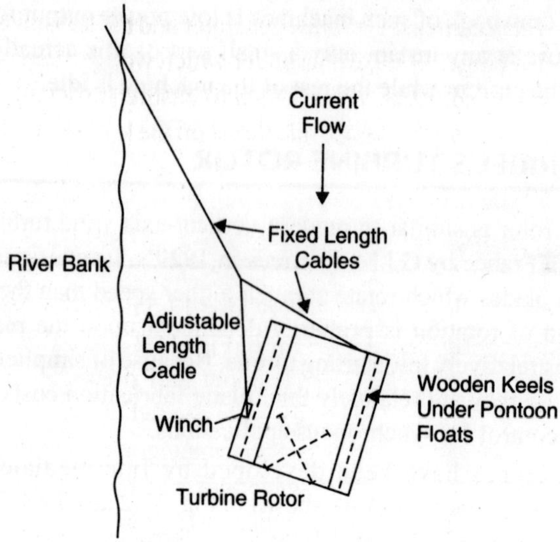

Fig. 11.4. Mooring system for first prototype

The Darrieus turbine rotor is a low speed machine. It is a low solidity device which is completely submerged during operation and this, together with its high efficiency (above 50%) means that a rotor of moderate size and modest materials content can extract useful amounts of energy from current speeds as low as 1m/s (2 knots).

Irrigation canals are expected to be an important area of application for floating type micro hydropower plants. In a large canal, the turbine rotor could be mounted on a pontoon as in a river situation, whereas on a small canal it might be cheaper to mount the rotor on a bridge or beam over the canal. The power output from the rotor could be increased by shaping the canal banks to form a venturi to increase the water velocity through the rotor.

The mooring details and site requirements are shown in Fig. 11.4 and 11.5 respectively. The mooring cable arrangement protects the rotor against submerged or semi-submerged objects striking the blades.

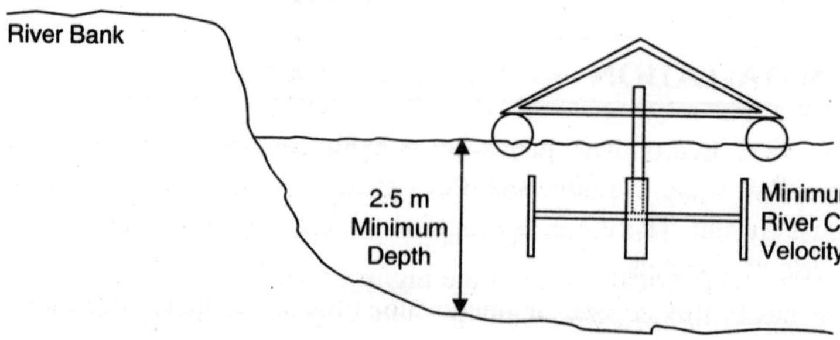

Fig. 11.5. Site requirement for turbine with 4 m^2 swept area

The pontoon which carries the turbine, generator and the transmission system, can float on two rows of barges or oil drums under which wooden keels are affixed. The mooring cable can be adjusted with a winch to ensure sufficient angle of the keels to the current direction so that water side thrust on the keels keeps the pontoon at a distance from the bank.

11.7 AUXILIARIES

The rotational speed of Darrieus turbine is very low: 13.5 rpm for vertical axis and 32 rpm for horizontal axis turbines as shown in Fig. 11.2 and 11.3. For Poncelet turbine, the peripheral velocity of runner is about half of water current speed. Therefore, multi-stage belt drives or gear boxes are needed to increase the speed of the generator shaft to about 950 rpm. Permanent magnet alternators or induction generators are preferred over synchronous generators. To reduce equipment costs, the conventional mechanical or hydromechanical speed governor should be dispensed with. The inertia of rotor being small, there is a problem of instability in power supply quality.

The above problems can be solved by use of a flywheel which can ensure stable power supply and can shave-off power demand fluctuations. A flywheel designed for this purpose can be accelerated to extremely high speeds without any risk of breaking apart. It can be made from concentric rings of quartz fibre as windings, the rings being fitted over one another and close gaps filled with an elastic substance to keep the plies of the rims together. The flywheel is coupled to a generator and enclosed in a sealed evacuated casing to reduce windage losses. The device operates as a generator when power demand on the system grows, and as an electric motor when it is time to accumulate energy. According to some calculations, the cost of 1 kW will be less than with pumped hydroelectric storage. A project has been described contemplating a 5 m diameter flywheel of 1.96 MN weight that could be charged to 20 MWh. The operating speed in 3500 rpm.

The mechanical energy storage system as described above can fit into appropriate technology level suitable for rural environment. The load governors based on electronic circutory or microprocessor technology may by able to solve the problem to some extent but may not be easily acceptable in rural areas because of higher levels of technology involved. Further, these load governors do not operate happily against unstable operation of turbine rotor. Load governors invariably require an auxiliary load or another hybrid system to store surplus electric power generated by hydel power plant during low demand period. This is not always a good decision thermodynamically, as electrical energy is the highest form of energy and hybrid systems help to degrade the energy form and in addition there are heavy conversion losses.

11.8 CONCLUSION

Floating type micro hydropower plants can be a very attractive proposition to harness enormous amounts of hydroenergy available as river current energy in the flat country side. Civil costs are reduced and reliable equipment can be developed for tapping the flow energy in the irrigation canals by constructing the banks into venturi shapes. Research and development efforts are needed to develop efficient turbine rotors working on the principle of wind turbines or old time water wheels followed by intensive field trials. The problem of stability and energy storage to improve load factors can be solved by the development of suitable flywheels. The development efforts must be constrained keeping in view the principles of appropriate technology suitable for harmonious development of rural areas involving local people, local materials and local resources.

11.9 REFERENCES

1. Peter German, '*The Development of a Turbine for Tapping River Current Energy*', Intermediate Energy Technology Development Group, London.
2. '*Upgrading and Further Development of Traditional Devices for the Utilisation of Hydro Energy*', Bremen Overseas Research and Development Association, Bremen.
3. Jagdish Lal, '*Hydraulic Machines*', Metropolitan Book Co. Pvt. Ltd., Delhi.
4. N.P. Cheremisinoff, '*Fundamentals of Wind Energy*', Ann Arbor Science Publishers Inc., Michigon, 1978.
5. P.D. Mohindra, '*Current from currents*', The Tribune, 14th June, 1982.
6. Brij Bhardwaj, 'Surplus Power by 1986 envisaged', Hindustan Times dated 5th April, 1984.
7. '*UP submits Five more Micro Hydel Schemes*', Hindustan Times dated 30th Sept., 1983.
8. Venikov and Putyatin, '*Introduction to Energy Technology*', Mir Publishers, Moscow, 1981.

Part 5
Wind Energy

Chapter 12

Wind Energy Utilization in Villages

12.1 SYNOPSIS

The importance of wind as an alternative source of energy will increase with the depletion of fossil fuels and the need to maintain our ecosystem. In many countries as well as in some parts of India, electric power is being commercially produced from windmills. There is a special need for lift irrigation in many parts of Haryana where surface water is scarce and topography does not permit effective flood irrigations by the canal system. Therefore, there is a large potential in these areas to exploit wind energy for pumping of surface and ground waters, especially to operate water sprinkler systems for irrigation.

This Chapter is based on the analysis of wind data for various parts of Haryana and study of technological feasibility of wind energy utilization for water pumping, taking into consideration the requirements of crops and availability of ground water. The Chapter also describes special research and development projects so that wind energy can be used in the near future in the plains of Haryana and other similar areas.

12.2 INTRODUCTION

The winds account for a power of 2×10^{13} W. Though this is only a small portion of the incident solar energy when compared, but it is more than the total energy consumption rate of the world. It is estimated that just one percent of potential wind power is equivalent to 2×10^{11} W or approximately three percent of the current world energy consumption rate. If wind power were used for the generation of electricity, its thermal equivalent would be as high as 8–9 percent of the total (Daniel M. Simmons 1975). Technical and economic problems related to the location and variability of wind intensity tend to limit the attractiveness of wind energy conversion systems, but the potential extractable wind power is not insignificant.

Following a better understanding of aerodynamics of rotating aerolifts, there is a revival of interest in harvesting wind energy. The importance of wind as alternative source of energy is increasing with the depletion of fossil fuels and the need to maintain our ecosystem. The Government of India has formulated and launched a special wind energy programme. At a conservative assessment, wind power potential in India is around 20000 MW (*The Hindustan Times*, New Delhi, 29 October 1992). At present, an aggregate wind power capacity of about 43 MW has been established in the country and it is proposed to establish an additional 100 MW capacity in the Eighth Plan. Although in many countries and some parts of India, electric power is being commercially produced from wind mills, wind energy can be more appropriately utilized for pumping water for irrigation due to high variation of power density of wind over time and location (Srivastava, Girija Sharma 1987). In India, windmills have been tried for pumping water for drinking, irrigation for fodder crops, forest nurseries, and agro-forestry plantations. But, so far, windmills have not been tried among individual farmers and in the irrigation of annually cultivated crops.

There is special need for lift irrigation in many parts of Haryana where surface water is scarce and topography does not permit effective flood irrigation by the canal system. Therefore, there is a large potential in these areas to exploit wind energy for pumping of ground water, especially to operate sprinkler systems.

12.3 WIND DATA

The average output of water from windmill pumping system must be matched with the requirements of various crop combinations and availability of ground water. Haryana is a small state (44212 sq km) with almost uniform topography (97 percent alluvial plains and three percent hilly tracts). Therefore, wind data have been compared for two typical tracking stations and is given in Table 12.1.

The examination of the wind speeds indicates that Haryana is a region of light breeze with wind speeds 6 to 11 kmph (1.6 to 3.3 k/s). The southern part of Haryana is slightly more favourable than the northern part.

The mean annual energy content of wind can be calculated as equal to 0.00001073 ρV_i; where V_i is the hourly wind speed in kmph for hour *i* and ρ is the mean air density equal, to 2.8703 kg/m^3. The mean annual energy content comes out to approximately 250 kWh/m^2.

Table 12.1. Mean daily wind speed data for Haryana

Month	*Mean daily wind speed (kmph)*	
	*Hisar**	*Karnal***
January	5.3	4.8
February	6.3	6.9
March	7.5	6.2
April	7.9	6.5

(Contd...)

Month	Mean daily wind speed (kmph)	
	*Hisar**	*Karnal***
May	8.9	7.4
June	10.7	7.8
July	9.9	4.8
August	7.7	4.7
September	6.7	4.9
October	5.5	4.5
November	4.7	4.3
December	5.4	5.4
Average	7.2	5.7

* Lat. 29° 10' N; Long 75° 44' E; Elev. 221 mast

** Lat. 29° 42' N; Long 77° 02' E; Elev. 249 mast

Source: Annamani, DA Modey, 1983. *Wind Energy Data for India.* Indian Institute of Tropical Meteorology, New Delhi: Allied Publishers Pvt. Ltd.

Table 12.2. District-wise ground water data for Haryana

District	*Utilizable recharge (ha-m)*	*Net draft (ha-m)*	*Pre-monsoon water level June, 1989 (m)*	*Post monsoon water level October, 1989 (m)*
Ambala	35054	30276	9.27	7.96
Yamunanagar	44089	41013	7.52	6.58
Kurukshetra	63648	51546	13.63	13.36
Karnal	121634	107426	8.24	8.00
Panipat	62162	47448	7.61	7.65
Sonipat	59855	24041	5.63	5.63
Faridabad	54605	20501	6.81	6.45
Kaithal	89768	61298	6.78	7.02
Jind	106689	20212	7.66	7.43
Rohtak	86905	16391	4.91	4.74
Gurgaon	46633	35440	9.15	8.91
Rewari	22591	15584	13.98	14.42
Sirsa	94110	17161	10.02	9.98
Hisar	120990	34557	9.28	9.35
Bhiwani	47900	13325	19.66	19.45
Mehenragarh	31902	22230	26.89	26.66
Average	—	—	10.44	10.22

Source: Ground water Directorate, 1990. *Ground water Monitoring in Haryana based on Observations during June, 1990–a technical report*. Haryana: Ground water Directorate.

12.4 GROUND WATER SITUATION IN HARYANA

The entire Haryana region has been surveyed for ground water availability by Ground water Directorate, Haryana State; and Minor irrigation and Tubewell Corporation, Karnal Districtwise ground water data are given in Table 12.2. The broad features of substantial parts of Haryana are promising from the point of used ground water potential. The irrigation requirements for Haryana are summarized as below (Singal 1985).

Drip irrigation for corn, wheat, cotton, millets = 25 m^3/ha-day
Flood irrigation for rice, sugarcane = 50–60 m^3/ha-day
Live stock = 40–50 litres/head-day
Lifting height = a few metres to 20 m.
Power required = 135 W/ha// for surface water;
400 W/ha for ground water

12.5 CHARACTERISTICS OF WIND TURBINES

Specific speed or tip-speed ratio of a windmill rotor is the ratio of its peripheral speed to wind speed. Rotors of low tip-speed ratio are preferred for driving piston pumps, which require a high starting torque and low rotational speed. The rotor of low tip-speed ratio also gives high efficiency and low cost. The other important characteristics of windmill rotors are cut-in speed and cut-out speed.

The main characteristics of windmills suitable for Haryana are given below:

1. It should be water pumping, low tip-speed ratio windmill preferably of vertical axis design.
2. It should be suitable for installation on open wells, canals, river beds, ponds, lakes, etc.
3. The total head over which water has to be lifted should be 15–20 m with suction head 10.5 m, if installed on ground level.
4. It should be suitable for rated wind speeds of 2 m/s with cut-in speed of 1.5 m/s.
5. Discharge at 2 m/s of wind speed and total head of 15 m should be 0.5 to 1 litre/s.
6. The system design should be suitable for operating a sprinkler system for irrigation.

The Windmill WP-2, developed at National Aeronautical Laboratory, Bangalore can pump 2.9 m^3/hour against a heat of 10 m at a wind speed of 3.5 m/s. A Sail Wind developed at the same laboratory uses six triangular canvas sails on a rotor of 7 m diameter and pumps 5.4 m^3/hour against a head of 10 m at wind speed of 3.5 m/s (Singal 1985).

The specifications of a propeller type windmill pump-set, which has been standardized for installation in India, are listed below:

Tower height	= 7 m
No. of propellers	= 12 m
Rotor Diameter	= 5m
Machine power ratio	= 0.36
Water depth	= 20 m
Maximum daily output	= 23 m^3 at a wind speed of 10 m/s.

The total cost of the machine including transportation and erection is ₹ 11750 and a similar expenditure is to be incurred on well-boring and construction of storage tank. The government provides a subsidy of ₹ 7500.

The wind-mills installed so far are not only of small size (about 5 m diameter), but also require high maintenance and support. Research and Development (R & D) efforts are now needed so as to reduce the maintenance expenditure of wind-mills to occasional oiling and changing the pump washer only. Somewhat larger wind-mills have to be developed than the presently available.

12.6 R & D EFFORTS NEEDED

The present windmill technology is inadequate for the low wind speed regions of Haryana. Special R & D projects in the following areas must be taken up so that wind energy can be used in near future in the plains of Haryana and other similar regions.

12.6.1 Artificial Winds

Generation of artificial winds to drive windmills by heating large surfaces with favourable thermodynamic properties is technically feasible. A project proposal has been prepared to heat a large surface in which case the resulting current (artificial wind) will drive turbines (Venikov. Putyatin 1981). The efforts needed to pursue the project in the form of money manpower, and time are huge.

12.6.2 Aeroelectric Plant

The low wind velocity in Haryana can be augmented by the use of diffusers at intake to windmills. Besides the propellers Madaras and Darrieus, there has been a plethora of designs for wind machines. One intriguing power plant design, called the aeroelectric plant, uses the flow up a tower that looks like a cooling tower (El-Wakil 1985). Its walls are heated by solar radiation. Since, the walls are circular, the sun's rays need not be tracked as it changes position in the sky during the day. The heated walls, in turn, heat the inside air and a flow up the tower is established. This air flow is made to drive a number of air turbines located near the top of the tower. The turbines, in turn, drive electric generators. The driving pressure causing air flow is given by the well-known chimney effect.

P. Carlson of California has proposed a slightly modified form in which, the interior air in a very tall tower would be cooled by pumping water to the top. The water evaporates in the low pressure air there, causing a downward flow of cooled air. The driving pressure can be calculated in a manner similar to that for wet cooling towers. A conceptual design of such a plant called for a 1.5 mi-high, 900 ft-diameter tower located in a hot desert and 10 wind turbines surrounding the tower periphery at the bottom producing 2500 MW. The above design can be scaled down for producing water pumping wind turbines in Haryana.

12.6.3 Low Wind Speed Turbines

The turbines available in India and abroad are suitable for a rated wind speed of 3.5 m/s or more whereas low wind speed turbines for rated values of 1.5–2 m/s are needed for Haryana. Special efforts are, therefore, needed to develop cheap and simple rotors, which can cut-in at low wind speeds available in Haryana.

The Savonius rotor and American multi-blade type windmills have optimum power coefficients at a very low tip-speed and can therefore be used as starting point to windmills suitable for low wind speeds. However, M/s H-Energiesysteman B.V. of Holland have developed twin blade propeller type rotors for low wind areas (wind speed less than 3 m/s) (The Netherlands Agency for Energy and Environment).

12.6.4 Energy Storage Schemes

A combination of a windmill and a micro-hydro turbine can be used for storage of energy as potential energy of water (Fig. 12.1). Water could be pumped to high reservoir during periods of high winds and the potential energy could then be used

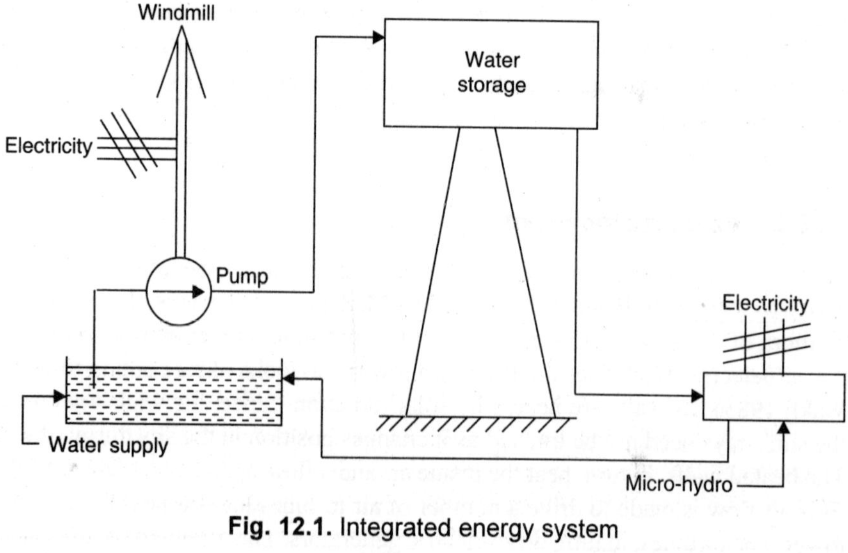

Fig. 12.1. Integrated energy system

during periods of low winds, assuming a constant output from the wind water generating system as the basis for sizing of the water generator and the storage system.

12.6.5 Windmill with Hydraulic Transmission

Hydraulic transmission consisting of a split fluid coupling/torque convertor can be used to run a centrifugal pump to lift deep ground water for the operation of a sprinkler system for irrigation (Fig. 12.2). The windmill is directly coupled to hydraulic pump part of coupling/torque convertor while hydraulic turbine part, which is directly coupled to the centrifugal water pump, is lowered deep in the open well. The variable speed/torque hydraulic pump sends pressure fluid through a pipe to drive the hydraulic turbine to operate the centrifugal pump.

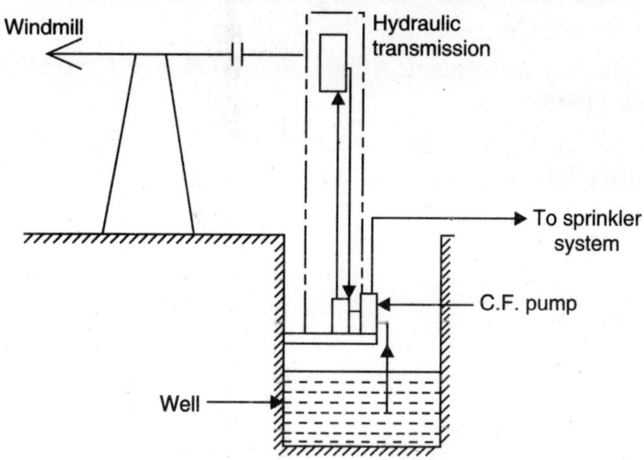

Fig. 12.2. Windmill with hydraulic transmission

The use of hydraulic transmission has many advantages such as optimum adaptation of rotor speed to guarantee a maximum output; no gear box; no controlling and switching equipment, as no electrical generator is involved; simple maintenance, as no reciprocating pump and allied crank mechanism; and the centrifugal pump can be installed on ground level or lowered into the deep open well to suit the suction lift available (The Ministry of Economic Affairs 1986).

12.7 CONCLUSIONS

Haryana has ample underground water to be tapped for irrigation. However, the wind characteristics are not favourable for the existing windmill technology. Special efforts are needed to develop suitable turbines and systems for adaptation in Haryana and other similar regions, so that abundant, reliable, clean wind can be harnessed cost-effectively as alternative and renewable source of energy to meet the irrigation and other requirements of plains of Haryana. It is recommended that a special research institute may be set up for carrying out the development projects.

12.8 REFERENCES

1. Daniel M. Simmons, *Wind Power*, Noyes Data Corporation, Park Ridge, New Jersey (1975).
2. *The Hindustan Times*, New Delhi, 29 October 1992.
3. R.K. Singal, *Non-conventional Energy for Lift lrrigation Electrical India*, vol. XXV: 8 (1985).
4. V.A. Venikov and E.V. Putyatin, *Introduction to Energy Technology*, Mir Publishers, Moscow (1981).
5. M.M. El-Wakil. *Power Plant Technology*, Mc Graw-Hill Book Company, New York, 1985, 624 pp.
6. The Netherlands Agency for Energy and Environment, *Holland Wind Energy*, Export Catalogue, 3503 RE Utrecht. 18 pp.
7. The Ministry of Economic Affairs, *Holland Energy*, Export Catalogue. The Hague (1986).
8. U.K. Srivastav and Girija Sharma, *Wind Energy for Water Pumping*, Oxford and IBH Publishing Co. Pvt. Ltd. New Delhi (1987).

Part 6
Biomass

Chapter 13

Fluidised Bed Technology for Rural Development

13.1 ABSTRACT

Fluidised bed technology has been utilized to carry out many diverse industrial processes. Examples of commercial or demonstrated applications range from metallurgical processes (roasting of ores), chemical reactions (catalytic cracking), combustion of low grade fuels, incineration, drying wet products, coal gasification, pneumatic transport of particulate matter, heat recovery and so on. But the capability of fluidised bed technology to burn low-grade fuels available in the rural areas with superior efficiency has opened out vast opportunities to meet the energy requirements for various socio-economic activities and development of rural areas.

The chapter discusses the rural energy and other requirements under Indian conditions and evaluates various applications of fluidised bed technology which can be utilized to meet them. The efforts being made at Regional Engineering College, Kurukshetra, in this direction have been highlighted.

13.2 INTRODUCTION

All organic materials, such as plants, trees and crops, are potential sources of energy and are collectively called biomass. The estimated production of agricultural residues in India is 200 million tonnes per year and that of wood is 130 million tonnes. At an average heating values of 18 MJ/kg db, a total potential of 6×10^{12} MJ/year or approximately 75×10^{7} MJ/hour exists. At a power conversion rate of 25 percent, total useful potential is about 75000 MW. This can supply all our villages with power at a rate of 30000 kWh per day per village against the present meagre consumption of only 150 kWh per day per village. With the availability of sufficient energy, there will be boost in agricultural production resulting in availability of morc biomass for energy recover and hence, the process is self-adjusting.

The versatility of fluidised bed combustion technology can be utilised for the efficient combustion of forestry and agricultural waste materials such as sawdust, wood chips, hog fuel, rice husk, straws, nutshells and pits[1]. The fluidised bed may be used in an air heater, liquid-phase heater (hot water or hot oil system) or a steam generator for process heat or power generation. Another method of utilization is pyrolysis of biomass in a fluidised bed gasifier to produce combustible gas for cooking, heating or power generation. This can also be used to run the engines of farm machinery and vehicles.

Various systems of fluidised bed technology which can be utilised for rural development are discussed in the following paragraphs.

13.3 FLUIDISED BED SYSTEMS

13.3.1 Biomass Combustion Systems

When solid particles are kept in a fluid state through contact with a gas, the best combustion results are achieved with combustion efficiency as high as 95–98 percent. This is done by keeping a bed of sand in a floating state by a certain quantity of air at a predetermined velocity and then heating the sand in this state to a temperature of about 550°C to 600°C. At this temperature, the required quantity of biomass is fed through a screw conveyor and the bed temperature is maintained in the region of 850°C by equal extraction of heat by the inbed heat exchanger. Heat input is kept under control by the rate of fuel feed. The heat thus released is absorbed in two zones — by the inbed tube heat exchanger and the conventional heat exchanger in the radiation/convection zone.

Fluidised bed combustion technology had the ability to burn a wide range of materials and can burn a combination of fuels or wastes in one unit. This versatility arises from the turbulent motion and large thermal inertial of the fluidised bed which enables the combustor to withstand the initial cooling action of fuels, particularly those high in ash and moisture as they enter the bed. This is typical characteristic of biomass. Agricultural wastes can be fed directly without any preparation with the exception of nutshells which should be crushed.

Low bed temperature (about 850°C) results in negligible NO_x emissions and no clinker formation. This low combustion temperature prevents fusion of ash and minimizes effects of fouling and erosion of heat transfer surface. The ash is clean and inert and may be used as landfill or in concrete. Fluidised bed of sand and fuel acts as a 'Thermal Flywheel' releasing heat whenever called for and responds very quickly to changes in load. Design of fluidised bed combustion system can ensure excellent Time-Temperature-Turbulence conditions for the complete and efficient combustion of biomass resulting in a compact, low cost furnace to meet the process heat requirements of small and cottage industries. The technology can be used as effectively for giant plants as for very small systems.

Following small plants based on fluidised bed technology can be developed for rural applications.

(*i*) Small steam generators or packaged boilers to produce steam for power generation or process heat for agro industries and other village industries.

(*ii*) Stand alone external furnaces to produce hot water for domestic applications or cottage industries or air for crop drying.

(*iii*) Thermic Fluid Heaters for village industries.

The steam generated in the boiler can be used to drive a turbine for power generation, or an engine to run a pump or a machine, or to operate a jet pump or steam refrigeration for domestic or commercial food preservation or milk chilling and processing, space heating, parboiling and other process heating in agro and food processing industries. The flue gas or hot air generated can be used for crop drying, timber drying, cement and brick industries or pneumatic transport of crops from fields to warehouses for storage or packing. The detailed applications are given in Table 13.1.

Table 13.1. Applications of Fluidised Bed Systems

FB System and output system	*Bottoming Plant*	*Applications*
Boiler-steam	Turbine	Electric power for domestic, community, irrigarion, food chain, village industries.
	Jet pump	Domestic and irrigation water.
	Steam refrigeration	Domestic and industrial food preservation, cooling, milk chilling.
	Steam	Process and space heating, parboiling, precooking.
Boiler-hot water	Hot water	Domestic, industries, laundary.
Thermic fluid heater	Hot oil	Industries.
Furnace-hot air	Dryer	Crop drying, industrial drying, timber, bricks, cement, pneumatic transport.
Gasifier-fuel gas	Stoves	Cooking.
	Gas turbine	Power for domestic, industries, community.
	Engine	Farm and local vehicles, farm machinery.
	Furnace	Foundary, forge, industrial heating.
	Synthesis	Chemical industries.

13.3.2 Gasifiers

Gasifiers are used to produce fuel gas from feed stocks such as wood, biomass or refuse. Gasification process involves heterogeneous gas-solid chemical reactions, which require substantial amounts of heat and mass transfer, and the problem posed in the design and development of plant to carry out these processes have led to a variety of types of gasifiers. An oxygen donor gasifier commercial plant is shown in Fig. 13.1. Various applications of fuel gas are also marked on the diagram[2].

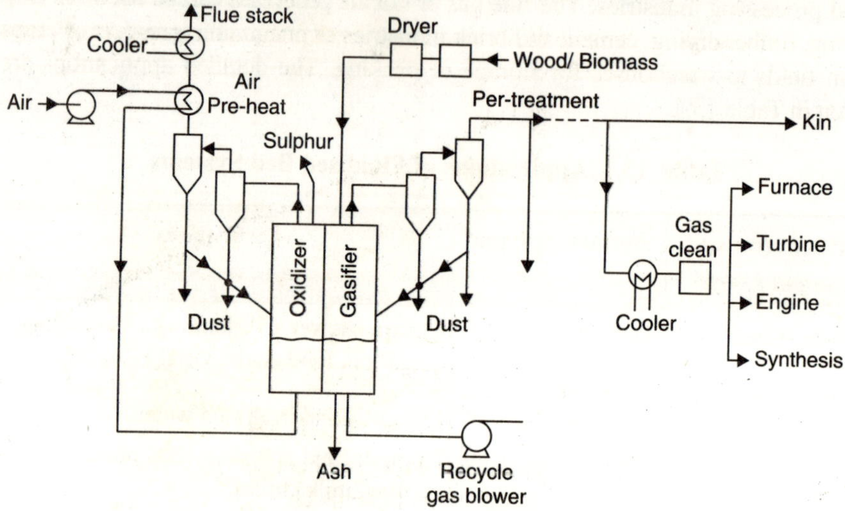

Fig. 13.1. Biomass gasifier

13.3.3 Dryers

Moist substances may be dried by passing hot and dry gases through the damp material. Irrespective of whether or not the material to be dried is fluidisiable, a supply of hot, relatively dry gas is needed. In some cases, the product to be dried will tolerate being dried by hot gases from combustion processes, whereas other products are less tolerant and require uncontaminated gas such as clean hot air. Fluidised bed furnaces are being developed as hot gas generator for crop drying, cement manufacture, etc. Such furnaces can provide hot combustion products or clean hot air. The source of the hot dry gas should be a separate entity from the dryer itself and of course has to be matched to the dryer.

Several types of dryers and process design are possible using fluidization techniques. Crops of granular materials (grains, pulses, seeds) can be fluidised and good particle/gas contact is possible. Fluidised bed dryers with relatively gentle handling and lack of moving parts make them attractive. A continuous 'plug flow' fluid bed dryer with straight path or reversing path or spiral path can be developed to adjust the residence time of the wet feed in the dryer.

13.3.4 Solids Transport System

Transport of grains from fields to warehouses or from point to point in agrobased industries can be achieved using fluidization techniques. In addition to solid conveying systems biomass can be fed into fluidised bed system by employing pneumatic conveying system.

13.4 RURAL ENERGY REQUIREMENTS

The development, welfare and prosperity of rural villages require cheap and abundant energy for domestic cooking food production and processing, heating and lighting, community development, irrigation water, mechanized agriculture and small village industries. The present status can be judged from the energy balance of Indian village. Pura given in Table 13.2.

Table 13.2. Energy Balance of Village Pura (3)

Source/Application	*Agriculture*	*Domestic*	*Lighting*	*Industry (in percent)*	*Total*
Fuel (wood, kerosene, electricity)	0.7	92.7	2.4	4.2	100
Muscle power (men, animal)	26.8	66.7	0	6.5	100
Total	2.8	90.6	2.2	4.4	100

13.4.1 Domestic Requirements

Eighty percent of the basic energy needs of rural India is the provision of cooking energy, which amounts to 0.5 to 1 kWh/person/day. It is mostly met from traditional fuels like fire wood and cowdung cakes. Cooking usually takes place on simple fire-places which have thermal efficiency of the order of just 5 percent. In areas where fuel wood is scarce, dung and agricultural residues are used. Fuel gas from a gasifier can be used for cooking.

Other domestic energy requirements for a model village are shown in Table 13.3. The traditional energy inputs and potential areas of substitution by fluidised bed systems are also marked in the table.

Table 13.3. Domestic Energy Requirements

Requirement	*Traditional methods*	*Potential FB system*
Cooking	wood, dung, agro residues	fuel gas from gasifier
Lighting	kerosene	electricity from local power plant
Hot water	wood, dung, agro residues	hot water boiler
Space heating	nil	steam heating, air heating
Cooling, refrigeration	nil	local power, steam refrigeration

13.4.2 Community Development

There is virtually no energy input for community life at present. Street lights, schools, hospitals, community halls can be provided with power supply from small power plants run on steam or gas from fluidised bed combustors or gasifiers fed with biomass.

13.4.3 Agriculture

More than 50 percent of agricultural energy can be attributed to animal power. Irrigation possibilities are limited and very premitive technologies are used for food processing, its storage, preparation and transport. The potential applications of F.B. Technologies for agriculture and food processing are given in Table 13.4.

Table 13.4. Agriculture and Food Chain

Requirement	*Traditional methods*	*Potential FB system*
Irrigation and Drainage	Draught animals	local power, jet pump-sprinkler system
Thrashing	Muscle power	local power
Drying	Open sun	local power
Milling	Muscle power	hot air crop dryer
Processing	Grid power. diesel	local power, steam for dehydration, freezing, precooking, parboiling, salting, pickling, smoking, fermentation, canning, bottling, packing, milk chilling.
Local transport	Muscle power, diesel	pneumatic conveying, fuel gas fired vehicles
Storage and marketing	natural ventilation	steam refrigeration/space heating, steam ejectors, ventilation fans.

13.4.4 Industry

Small power plants and steam generators and gasifiers are urgently needed to supply power and steam for preservation of food in cold storages and milk chilling plants cottage and village industries using lathes, looms, workshops, furnaces, foundaries, parboiling, heating, etc. The fluidised boilers or gasifiers can work in conjunction with various cycle configurations using steam turbines, gas turbines, combined cycles, with and without co-generation of thermal loads to produce electricity, steam hot water, hot air, hot oil etc.

13.5 DESIGN OF A RURAL POWER PLANT

A project on the design of a rural power plant based on fluidised bed combustion system for biomass was undertaken at Regional Engineering College, Kurukshetra. The salient features of the project are described below:

13.5.1 Survey Data of Village 'BIROHAR' in District Kurukshetra

Total population	: 3000
No. of houses	: 400
Area under cultivation	: 1200 acres
Wheat and Rice	: 500
Sugar cane	: 400
Mustrad	: 200
Miscellaneous	: 100
Method of irrigarion	: 100 pumps of 7.5 hp each with sprikler system
Other Electrical Loads	:
Flour mills	: 2 × 10 hp
Domestic flour mill	: 100 × 2.5 hp

(Also used for shredding of cattle feed in addition to milling).

Thrasher	: 20 × 10 hp.

13.5.2 Biomass Availability

Saw dust, wood chips, etc from saw mill	: 3t per day
Agricultural residues from wheat and mustard	
Crop @ 1.6 t/acre/year	: 320t per year
Rice husk	: 800t per year
Baggage (dried @ 2t/acre)	: 800t per year

Total biomass available : 7.5t per year

Total biomass required for the proposed plant of 3 MWt capacity based on 35 percent overall efficiency and biomass heating value of 35 kcal/kg is 25t per day. Therefore, it is required to collect the additional requirement from the surrounding village or undertake special fuel crop plantation.

Agricultural residues are seasonal depending upon the crop. However, some overlay, and with properly managed storage areas, a fairly uniform feed supply can be ensured. The biomass can be stored in an enclosed area of 15 m × 15 m with a heap height of 6 m. This is worked out on the basis of 60 days inventory and bulk density of biomass of 150 kg/m^3. A shredding machine may be required to keep the feed size to 6 cm.

The biomass, sized and dried, is fed to the combustion chamber through belt conveyors and screw feeder 25 cm diameter × 16 m long driven by 1.5 hp motor. The feed control is automatically affected by regulating the speed of the motor. A 600 mm rotary valve is used to feed biomass to the combustor under pressure.

A schematic diagram of a Rural Power Plants is shown in Fig. 13.2.

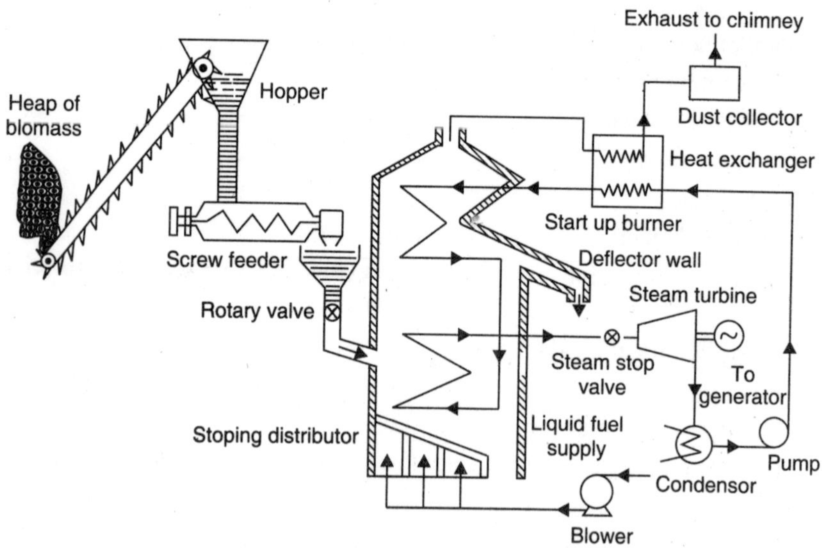

Fig. 13.2. Rural power plant

13.5.3 Proposed Focal Village

(*i*) Industrial Estate

Saw mill	:	10 hp
Toy making machine	:	10 hp
Milk chilling plant	:	20 hp
Rice mill	:	20 hp

	Repair workshop	:	50 hp
	Flour mill	:	20 hp
(ii)	Agricultural Load		
	Irrigation pump-sets		
	100 × 7.5 hp	:	750 hp
	Thrashers	:	20 hp
(iii)	Domestic Load		
	Fans, lighting, radio and		
	TV sets. 400 × 500 W	:	200 kW
	Domestic flour mills		
	100 × 1.5 kW	:	150 kW
(iv)	Community Load		
	Street lights 50 × 40 W	:	2 kW
	Hospital and Community		
	Centre, school	:	16 kW
(v)	Total connected load	:	1000 kW
	Required installed capacity		
	with diversity factor 1.5	:	660 kW

13.5.4 Plant Specifications

Capacity	: 3 MWt
Plant	: Recirculation type
Biomass (mixture of saw dust, baggage, rice husk crop residues)	: 25t/day
Reactor size	: 1.4 m dia × 1.4 m bed height
Bed material (lined with fire bricks)	: 2.8t of 16 mesh sand
Fluid air	: 3.65 kg/sec at a velocity of 2 m/sec.
Fluid air system	: Roots blower 2.86 m^3/sec discharge and 1.9 bar pressure with 500 hp motor.
Parasitic power requirements of power plant	: 340 kW
Total plant capacity	: 1000 kWe

Distributor plate

Three compartments for differential velocities to ensure circulation of sand and biomass inside the furnace. The minimum velocity through sieve is 2m/sec and velocities in the three chambers are 2.4 m/sec., 2.8 m/sec. and 3.2 m/sec.

Dust collection system

A cyclone separator is provided after the heat recovery unit and before the stack to remove dust particles. The cyclone separator with 98% efficiency will be 1150 mm diameter and 2300 m height.

Steam tubes

Ceramic tubes of silicon carbide with 5 fins per inch (disk type), 80 mm diameter and 1.6 mm thick. 23 U-tubes of 1500 mm length will be required.

Steam parameters for steam turbine plant

Superheated steam of 20 bar and 275°C. Flow rate: 27t/hour

13.5.5 Automatic Control and Interlocking

The aim of control system is to meet the variable load demand effectively. The main requirements are:

(*i*) to maintain highest combustion efficiency

(*ii*) to regulate air supply in fluidised bed

(*iii*) to control fuel feed

(*iv*) to control steam flow rate.

The controlling parameter used is steam pressure which is used to control feedwater rate, fuel supply rate and air quantity. Electrical system is used for transmitting the signals to water control valve, fuel feed motor and blower damper.

13.6 FINAL COMMENTS

The whole of rural energy and other requirements of a village can be met from locally available biomass that would otherwise be wasted. This can be achieved by utilizing fluidised bed technology.

Throughout its history, fluidised bed technology has developed largely from experimentation. The design of fluidised bed plant is likely to continue to be sometime of an art and rely considerably upon observed behaviour and data obtained from previously constructed plant or pilot plant. It is not amenable to mathematical analysis.

In order to exploit the vast potential of fluidised bed systems for rural development and to overcome the inherent complexity of the real processes and caution to be exercised in applying the technology to specific cases, following projects have been undertaken at Regional Engineering College, Kurukshetra sponsored by the Ministry of Human Resource Development. Government of India, to build pilot plants for experimentation and collection of data to develop commercial plants for rural development.

(*i*) A pilot plant for research and development of a fluidised bed system for combustion of agro residues.

(*ii*) A pilot plant for the development of a hot air generator and grain dryer for agrobased and food processing industries.

13.7 REFERENCES

1. M. J. Cook, '*Fluidised Bed Combustion for Burning Biomass*', International conference on Fluidised Combustion: Is it achieving its promise? 16/17 October, 1984, London.
2. J. R. Howard, '*Fluidised Bed Technology: Principles and Applications*', Adam Hilger, Bristol and New York, 1989.
3. Energy use and Energy Conservation in Less Developed Countries—A Report by B & G Consultants, Netherlands.
4. R. K. Singal, '*Rural Energy: Design of a Fluidised Bed Combustion System for Biomass*', Electrical India, 15th April, 1988.

Chapter 14

Design of Combustion System

14.1 INTRODUCTION

Steam power plants and nuclear power plants are essentially base-load power plants which can give their best performance by continuous operation at their rated capacities. Intermittent running at reduced loads would result in higher heat rates due to off-design operation of equipments at their lower efficiencies and higher rates of parasitic consumptions per unit generated. The capacity factor is also adversely affected by the loss of reliability and availability of the plant due to enhanced failure rates as a result of thermal fatigue of the equipments. In addition to the in-plant measures, the plant capacity can be improved by higher load factors of the consumers.

The centralzonal power grids connecting coal based thermal plants, nuclear and hydropower plants and work in more efficient and reliable manner at high load factors feeding power to industrial belts and high commercial centres only. Tremendous investments and huge power losses in the long and unwieldy power lines to remote and scattered villages can be saved. The whole of rural energy (of low load factors) can be supplied by small local power plants utilizing biomass fuel sources, current energy in the flowing waters of rivers and irrigation canals, supplemented by gadgets based on non-conventional sources of energy mainly solar energy.

The above scheme can result in energy conservation not only by reducing huge losses in power plant operation at below capacity factors and transmission lines but also by substitution of commercial energy sources with renewable energy sources like biomass, hydro, solar and the like which are going waste untapped at present.

A study project was undertaken to investigate the feasibility of application of fluidised bed combustion technology for clean and efficient burning of huge biomass locally available to meet the evergrowing rural energy needs of India in a continuous and renewable manner. The energy needs and biomass availability in a sample village have been estimated and major systems and components have been designed for a fluidised bed combustor adoptable to a steam power plant of one MW gross electrical output.

The fluidised bed units can be used in conjunction with various configurations of power cycles using Rankine, Brayton and combined cycles. The ever increasing potential of biomass can be tapped to bring prosperity to rural India. In the bargain, the performance of central power stations can be improved by isolating low-load-factor rural consumers and there will be appreciable energy conservation through substitution.

14.2 ENERGY NEEDS

The average energy consumption of Indian villages is 150 kWh per day for energizing irrigation pumps, lighting, cooking, etc. The capacity of the power plant to meet the energy requirements of the village is based on a typical village 'BIROHAR' in District Kurukshertra. A survey was conducted for the existing power consumption in the village and the data was used to work out power required for a focal village. This survey also included the amount of biomass locally available.

14.2.1 Survey Data

Total population	:	3000
No. of houses	:	400
Area under agriculture	:	1200 acres.

Name of the Crop		Area under cultivation (acres)
Wheat and Rice	:	500
Sugar cane	:	400
Mustard	:	200
Miscellaneous	:	100

The whole of the land is irrigated with pumps. The number of pumps are 100 having electric motors of 7.5 hp and use sprinkler system.

There are two flour mills of 10 hp each and approximately 100 domestic flour mills of 2.5 hp each which are also used for shredding of cattle feed in addition to milling of flour. There are 20 thrashers of 10 hp each.

14.2.2 Proposed Focal Village

(*i*) Industrial Park

Saw mill	: 10 hp
Toy making machine	: 10 hp
Milk chilling plant	: 20 hp
Rice mill	: 20 hp

Repair work shop	: 50 hp
Flour mill	: 20 hp
(*ii*) Agricultural load	
Irrigation pump sets	
100 @ 7.5 hp	: 750 hp
Thrashers	: 20 hp
(*iii*) Domestic load	
400 houses @ 500 W (including fans, lighting, radio and TV sets)	: 200 kW
Domestic flour mills	
100 @ 1.5 kW	: 150 kW
(*iv*) Community load.	
Street lights 50 tubes @ 40 W	: 2 kW
(*v*) Hospital and community centre	: 16 kW
Total connected load	: 1000 kW
Diversity factor	: 1.5 kW
Required installed capacity	: 660 kW
Parasitic power requirements of the Fluidised Bed Unit and power plant	: 340 kW
Total plant capacity	: 1000 kW

14.3 BIOMASS AVAILABILITY

All organic materials, such as plants, trees and crop residues are potential sources of energy and are collectively called biomass. The estimated production of agricultural residues in India is 200 million tonnes per year and that of wood is 130 million tonnes. At an average heating value of 18 MJ/kg db, a total potential of 6×10^{12} MJ per year exists. At a power conversion rate of 35 percent, total useful potential is about 75000 MW. This can supply all our villages with power at a rate of 30000 kWh per day per village against the present meagre consumption of only 150 kWh per day per village. With electrification of the irrigation pumps, there will be a boost in agricultural production resulting in availability of more biomass for energy recovery and hence the process is self-adjusting.

The amount of biomass locally available in the village 'BIROHAR' was found to be as follows:

Saw dust wood chips, etc. from the saw mill	:	3t per day.
Agricultural residues from wheat and mustard crop @ 1.6t/acre/year	:	320t per year.
Rice husk	:	800t per year.
Baggage (dried) @ 2t/acre	:	800t per year.
Total biomass available	:	7.5t per day.

Total biomass required for the proposed power plant based on % overall efficiency and biomass heating value of 3500 kcal/kg is 25t/day. Therefore, it is required to collect the additional biomass from the surrounding villages.

14.4 STORAGE MANAGEMENT AND FUEL FEEDING SYSTEM

Agricultural residues are seasonal depending upon the crop. However, some overlay, and with properly managed storage areas, a fairly uniform feed supply can be ensured. The biomass can be stored in an enclosed area of 15 m × 15 m with a heap height of 6 m. This is worked out on the basis of 60 days' inventory and bulk density of biomass of 150 kG/m^3. A shredding machine may be required to keep the feed size up to 6 cm.

The biomass, sized and dried, is fed to the combustion chamber through belt conveyors and screw feeder 25 cm diameter × 16 m long with 1.5 hp motor. The feed control is automatically affected by regulating the speed of the motor. A 600 mm rotary valve is used to feed biomass to the combustor under pressure.

14.5 PLANT SPECIFICATIONS

Capacity	:	3 MW
Type	:	Recirculation type to suit biomass properties.
Biomass (mixture of saw dust, baggasse, rice husk, crop residues, etc.)	:	25t/day
Fluid air	:	3.65 kg/sec at a velocity of 2m/sec.
Size	:	1.4 m dia × 1.4 m bed height.
Bed lined with fire bricks	:	2.8t of 16 mesh sand
Fluid Air System	:	Roots blower 2.86 m^3/sec discharge and 1.9 bar pressure with a motor of 500 hp.

The distributor plate under the furnace is divided into three compartments for dicerential velocities to get circulation of sand and biomass inside the furnace. The minimum velocity in the furnace through siece is 2 m/sec and velocities in three chambers are 2.4 m/sec, 2.8 m/sec.

Dust collection system. A cyclone separator is provided after the heat recovery unit and before the stack to remove the dust particles. The cyclone separator with 98% collection efficiency will be 1150 mm diameter and 2300 mm height.

Steam Tubes: Ceramic tubes of silicon carbide with 5 fins/inch (disk type); 80 mm diameter and 1.6 mm thick. Twenty three U-tubes of 1500 mm length will be required.

Steam parameters for the steam turbine plant: Superheated steam at 20 bar and 275°C. Mass flow rate 2.7t/hour.

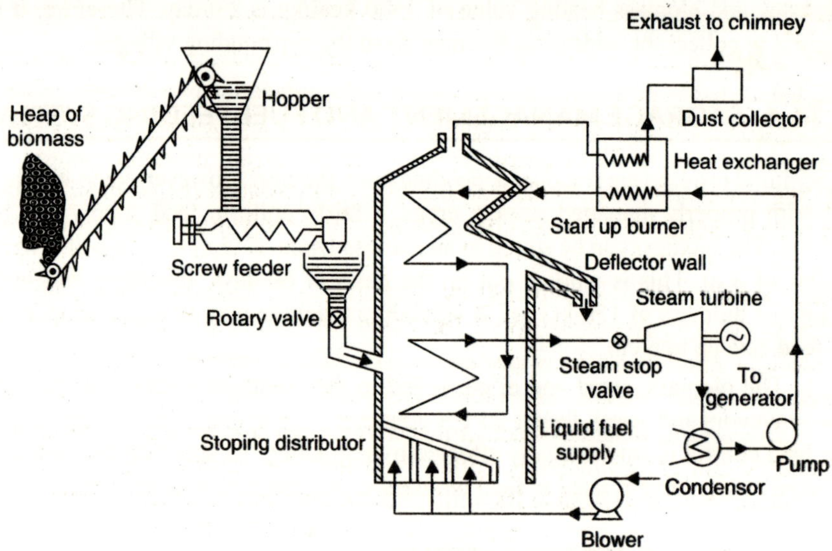

Fig. 14.1 Rural power plant

14.6 AUTOMATIC CONTROL AND INTERLOCKING

The aim of control system is to meet the variable load demand effectively. The main requirements are:

(*i*) to maintain highest possible combustion efficiency.

(*ii*) to regulate air supply in fluidised bed.

(*iii*) to control fuel supply.

(*iv*) to control steam flow rate.

The controlling parameter used in steam pressure which is used to control feed water rate, fuel supply rate and air quantity. Electrical system is used for transmitting the signals, to water control valve, fuel control valve and blower damper.

Chapter 15

Power Cycles for Rural Energy

15.1 INTRODUCTION

India is a peculiar country with 564276 small and big village remotely scattered and widely dispersed all over the land. Most of the population lives in these villages and depends upon agricultural sector for their livelihood. On the average, these villages need 150 kWh of energy per day for energizing irrigation pumps, for lighting, for cooking etc. As the load factor is very low and because these villages are widely dispersed, it is most uneconomical to electrify them from power grids. It is equally difficult to reach them with fossil fuels. If locally available energy sources could be converted to electrical power to drive irrigation pumps, the rural scene in India would change appreciably, and it would help to boost agricultural production which is vitally important to raise the standard of living of growing population.

All organic materials, such as plants, trees and crops, are potential sources of energy and are collectively called biomass. The estimated production of agricultural residue in India is 200 million tonnes per year and that of wood is 130 million tonnes. At an average heating value of 18 MJ/kg db, a total potential of 6×10^{12} MJ/year or approximately 75×10^{7} MJ/hour exists. At a power conversion rate of 35 percent, total useful potential is about 75000 MW. This can supply all our villages with power at a rate of 30,000 kWh per day/village against the present meagre consumption of only 150 kWh per day per village. With electrification of the irrigation pumps, there will be a boost in agricultural production resulting in availability of more biomass for energy recovery and hence, the process is self-adjusting.

Some thought has been given to chemical treatment of certain crop residues to make them acceptable for animal feed. There are certain residues, such as sugar beet pulp and hops from breweries, that can be dehydrated and used as animal feed without further treatment. Keeping aside 40 million tonnes for commercial sector for production of chemical feeds, fodder, roofing material, composting and other needs, it appears that a substantial amount of residue is available as fuel. If it is burnt in an uncontrolled manner, it presents a serious environmental problem besides loss of huge amount of recoverable energy. Biomass residues because of their low bulk density and extensive smoke formation are the most inconvenient and pollutant fuel for direct combustion. Collection and transportation problems prohibit the centralised use of residues. Agricultural wastes are seasonal, depending on the crop. However, some overlap and with properly managed storage areas, a fairly uniform feed supply could be available. Local power plants serving one large village or a group of smaller villages are feasible.

The purpose of this chapter is to describe some power cycles for thermal energy recovery from collectable crop residues in the agricultural and forestry states and to prepare an independent power system for rural areas consisting of local power plants burning biomass.

The central/zonal power grids connecting coal based thermal plants, nuclear and hydro plants can work in more efficient and reliable manner at high load factors feeding power to industrial belts and big commercial centres. Tremendous investments and huge power losses in the long and unwieldy power lines to remote and scattered villages can be saved.

The whole of rural energy can be supplied by local small power plants utilizing the biomass fuel sources that would otherwise be wasted. The development, welfare and prosperity of rural population can be enhanced by making available abundant and cheap energy for domestic cooking, heating and lighting, community development, irrigation water, mechanised agriculture and small industrial parks based on local resources.

15.2 COMBUSTION OF BIOMASS

Various combustion techniques are available for burning biomass, the most suitable depending upon actual application. The selection of most suitable combustion equipment will depend on properties, such as chemical analysis, volatile content, calorific value, particle size and ash characteristics, as well as the specific application. However, the versatility of the fluidized bed combustion makes it a strong candidate in many cases. A great deal of work is now being done on various fluidised bed concepts. This concept may be used for the efficient combustion of forestry and agricultural waste materials, such as sawdust, wood chips, hog fuel, rice husks, straws, nutshells and pits. The fluidized bed may be used in an air heater, liquid-phase heater or steam generator. It offers interesting possibilities in efficient energy recovery. When fired directly into a boiler, stream can be generated for process or power. Another method of utilization is pyrolysis. In this process, material is converted into a combustible gas that can be fired into a boiler or combustion chamber of a gas turbine. The ash is clean and inert and may be used as landfill or in concrete.

With fluidised bed combustion, the fuel is fed into a bed of hot inert particles, such as sand kept in fluidised state with air at sufficient velocity from below. The operating temperature is normally controlled within the range 750–950°C. Ideally it is kept as high as possible in order to maximize the rate of combustion and heat transfer but low enough to avoid problem of sintering of the bed particles. The rapid mixing and turbulence within the fluidised bed enables efficient combustion to be achieved with high heat releases as well as effective transfer, than in conventional boilers. This can result in more compact boiler with less tubing.

A major advantage of fluidised bed combustion is that, because of the low temperatures involved, there is a great potential for reducing and controlling atmospheric pollution. Nitrogen oxides are not formed from the nitrogen in the air and emission of many of the trace elements associated with fuels are less than those obtained using alternate combustion techniques.

Fluidised bed combustion technology has the ability to burn a wide range of materials and can burn a combination of fuels or wastes in one unit. This versatility arises from the turbulent motion and large thermal inertia of the fluidised bed which enables the combustor to withstand the initial cooling action of fuels, particularly those high in ash and moisture as they enter the bed. This is typical characteristic of biomass. Agricultural wastes can be fired directly without any preparation with the exception of nutshells, which should be crushed.

15.3 DESIGN OF FLUIDISED BED COMBUSTION SYSTEM

Properties of some biomass fuels are given in Table 15.1. The chemical composition and physical form of the biomass will influence the design of the fluidised bed combustion system. As compared to coal, the oxygen content of biomass is very high (about 40 percent) and contains much more volatiles and less fixed carbon. The stoichiometric air requirements will be quite different. The design of the fuel storage facilities, feeding arrangements and combustor equipment has to suit the higher volumetric feed rates necessary for biomass because of its generally low calorific value and density and to accommodate many shapes and size of biomass.

Table 15.1. Combustion Data on Biomass

Fuel Type	*Size mm*	*Bulk density Kg/m*	*Proximate Analysis*				
			Moisture % ar	*Ash % db*	*Volatile matter % db*	*Fixed carbon % db*	*Calorific Value MJ/kg db*
Rice husk	Ca 2	150	12	11	72	17	18
Corn cobs	200 × 25	190	8	<1	85	15	18
Baggasse	—	80	50	<1	80	20	19
RDF							
Shredded	—	130	16				
Pelletised	25	500		15	65	20	17
Wood							
saw dust	ca 2	160	20				
chips	ca 10	310		<1	80	20	20

ar: as received.

db: dry basis.

The high moisture content of biomass (up to 50 percent as received) and volatiles (up to 80 percent dry basis) give rise to some operational problems connected with controlling bed temperatures and avoiding excessive smoke production. The water in the fuel evaporates as it enters the bed, and this requires heat from the bed. The volatiles as released from the fuel tend to burn above the bed and do not provide heat for the bed itself. Therefore, relatively high fuel feed rates are needed to maintain bed temperature. However, with these high rates, incomplete combustion takes place with the limited oxygen provided by the fluidising air resulting in excessive smoke formation. This problem is aggravated with larger beds because of relatively poor lateral distribution of the fuel.

The best solution to this problem is to take steps to encourage combustion of volatiles in the bed by feeding the fuel directly into the bed and operating with high bed temperatures, relatively deep beds and fluidising velocities designed to promote good mixing and distribution of fuel throughout the bed. Provision of secondary air just above the bed can also be useful in reducing smoke emissions. Because biomass fuels have low densities, it is preferable to feed them as relatively large-sized pieces like corn cobs, wood chips, etc., into a bubbling fluidised bed, Fig. 15.1. The fuel is first metred through a rotary valve or screw feeder before being dropped onto the fluidised bed at only a few points, the number depending on the overall bed area. Bed turbulence distributes the fuel throughout the bed. The ash content of these fuels is low with ash being very fine and easily elutriated from the fluidised bed.

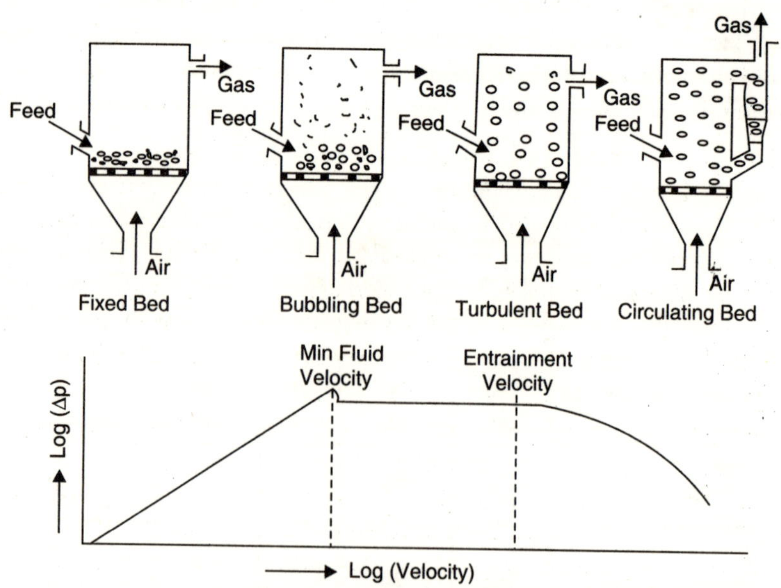

Fig 15.1. Types of fluidized beds

The finer feed stocks of biomass like rice husk and saw dust are difficult to burn satisfactorily in bubbling fluidized bed, because of excessive elutriation at the fluidising velocities needed for good mixing of the fuel in the bed. It is better to employ a circulating fluidised bed combustion system, Fig. 15.2, for very finely divided forms of biomass. This circulating bed is characterised by high fluidising velocities in excess of 3 m/s with entrainment of majority of bed particles which are collected by cyclone separator and returned to the combustor. The primary combustion air is fed through the main fluidising air distributor at the bottom while secondary air is introduced further up the reactor. Fine grains of sand are used as the bed materials.

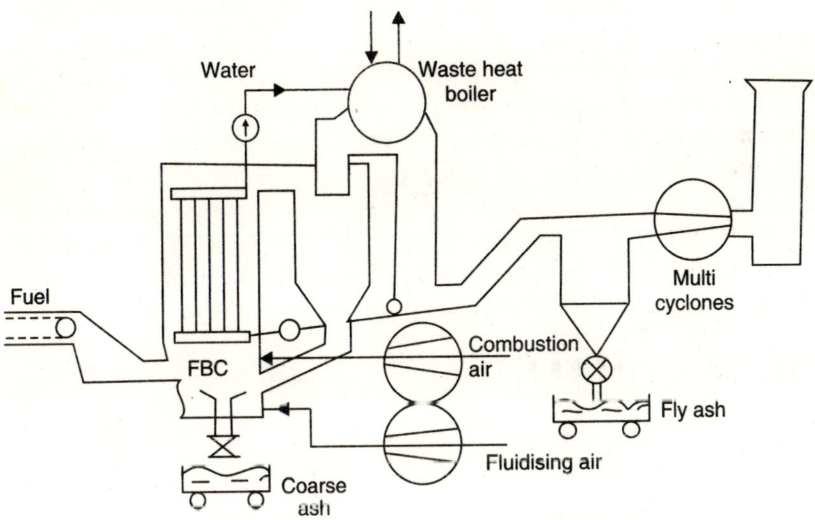

Fig. 15.2. Circulating bed boiler system

The fuel is screw-fed into the combustor which operates between 700°C and 1000°C, depending on the fuel being burned. Because the circulating material is in a highly turbulent state and mixes rapidly, bed temperatures remain very uniform. Boiler tubes are situated in the upper part of the combustor and downstream after the cyclone. It is a good system for burning biomass fuels with low density and small size which can be difficult to burn in more conventional 'bubbling' type of fluidised bed combustor.

The combustion of biomass in a fluidised bed requires that the bed be initially heated by means of a gas burner to a temperature of approximately 400°C. The gas burner is then shut off and biomass feed is started. The fuel ignites and from then on sustains combustion. In some cases, the bed remains hot enough to ignite the fuel directly without gas assist even after a shut down of over 24 hours. Coarse materials burn within the bed. Finer portions are carried through the bed and burn in the hot gases over the bed. Rocks and other non-combustible foreign materials are automatically removed from the bed on a continuous basis by extracting a portion of the bed material, screening out foreign matter, and reintroducing the bed material to the combustion unit. Biogas can be easily made available for initial heating of the bed.

Analysis of the overall heat transfer process for a tube immersed in a fluidised bed shows that the main resistance to heat flow is on the fluidised bed side of tube. Combination of fin designs and operating parameters have been evolved that lead to optimum performance. Ceramic tubes of silicon carbide in both plain and fined configuration are now commercially available. The bed material may be any clean, non-combustible material of uniform size. The system will require air clean-up equipment to satisfy air quality requirements of Air Pollution Control Board.

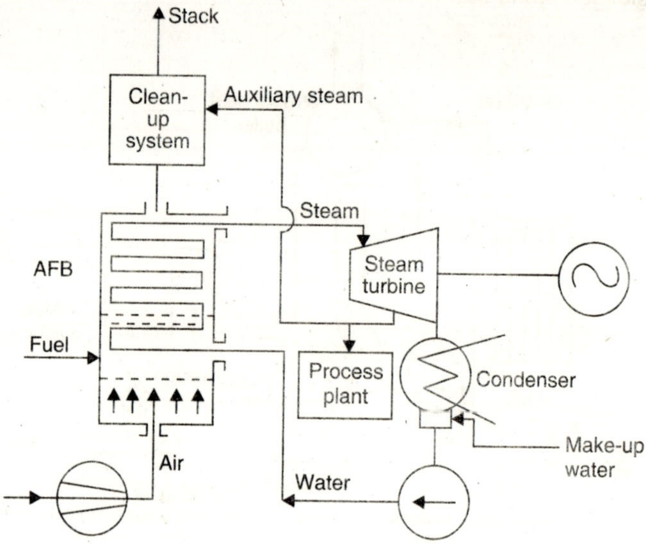

Fig. 15.3. Steam turbine cycle system (fluidised bed)

15.4 STEAM TURBINE CYCLE

Atmospheric fluidised bed (AFB) have been developed for combustion of biomass. This AFB is used in conjuction with a steam turbine, Fig. 15.3.

Heat is transferred to water by heat transfer surfaces within the bed, in the water-cooled walls, and in the convective space above the bed. Data on AFB boiler performance, cost and auxiliary electricity and steam requirements are available and quite differ from those of conventional steam turbine systems. A fuel conversion efficiency of 71 percent has been claimed. The technology is in the development stage, and these data should be updated whenever this system is considered.

15.5 GAS TURBINE CYCLES

An indirect-fired open-cycle system is shown in Fig. 15.4. The gas turbine combustor is replaced or operated in conjunction with a means for adding heat to the compressed air by air heat exchange tubes subjected to external firing in the fluidised bed unit. The system consists of five components: a fluidised-bed combustor, heat exchanger, a gas turbine generator set, cyclone separators, and emission control equipment (baghouse). A system as this requires a steam bottoming cycle for efficient operation. The exhaust from the fluidised bed is joined with the gas turbine exhaust, which is then used to generate high pressure, high temperature steam in a heat recovery boiler, which then powers a bottoming steam turbine in the normal manner. A primary gas clean-up system is installed after the fluidised bed to catch the larger ash particles before going to the boiler. Final clean-up can take place in the boiler by soot blowing and outside the boiler by cyclones and baghouses.

A separate air source is used for fluidisation to assure clean hot air for turbine operation. It some portion of compressor air is used for fluidisation, thorough clean up is required prior to joining the main air stream for introduction into gas turbine.

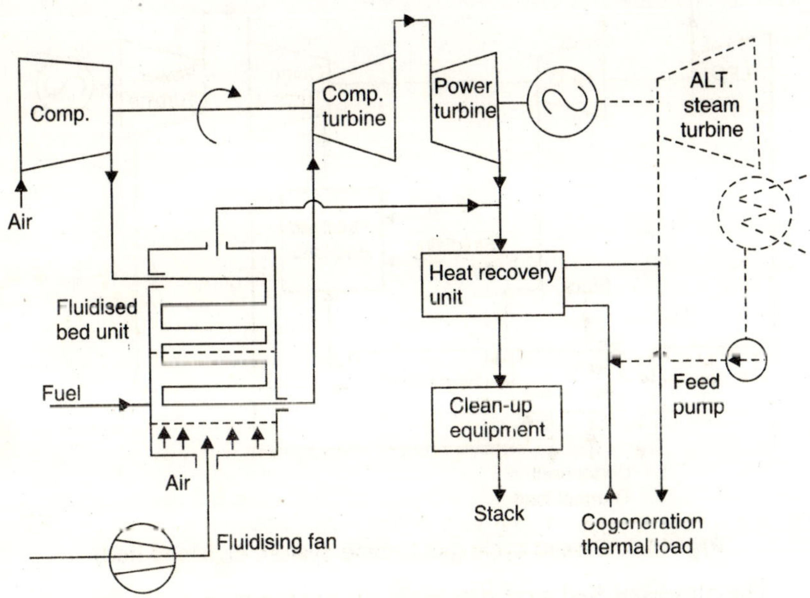

Fig. 15.4. Indirect-fired open-cycle gas turbine system (fluidised bed)

Heat transfer tubes used with fluidised bed system are both over the bed and immersed in the bed. Air from the compressor enters the over-bed tubes and proceeds down to the in-bed tubes, which operate at the highest temperature. Tube material is selected for both corrosion resistance on the outside and high temperature. Ceramic tubes are available with external extended surface rings. The control of the system is achieved by control of fuel as well as air supply. The latter should, however, never be less than that required to keep the bed in fluid state.

In the closed system, the working fluid (gas) flows under pressure through a compressor, heat exchanger, fluidised bed gas heater, gas turbine, again through the heat exchanger and then through the precooler back to the compressor inlet,

Fig. 15.5. The gas may be air, nitrogen or helium which is not in direct contact with the products of combustion. The heat rejected by the intercooler and precooler can be recovered by a secondary heat transfer loop to generate low pressure steam, to activate an absorption chiller for a cold storage or to produce additional power through an organic bottoming cycle. The cycle efficiency of a closed-loop gas turbine system is well above 42 percent. Control of system can be accomplished by passing air from the compressor discharge around the regenerator and to the turbine exhaust. While compressor power remains almost constant the turbine output decreases as a result of simultaneous decrease in turbine mass flow, expansion ratio and efficiency. The fluidised bed combustion unit will have both bed-immersed tubes and over-bed tubes.

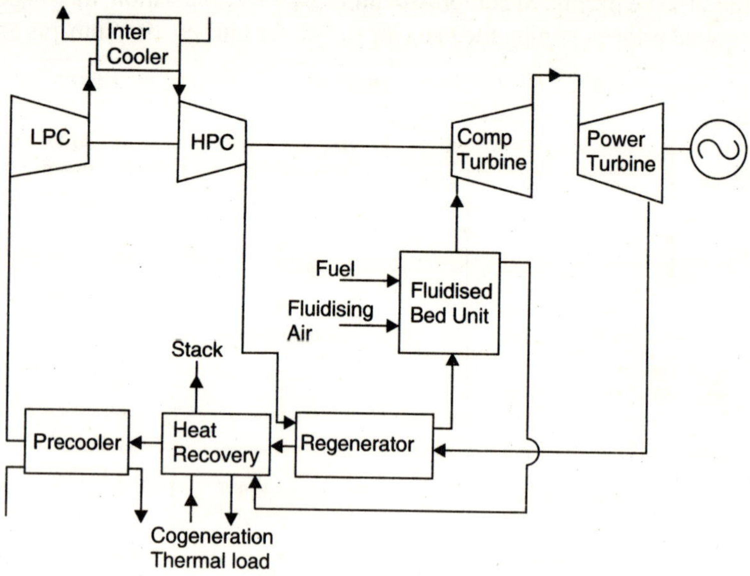

Fig. 15.5. Closed cycle gas turbine system (fluidised bed)

The fluidised bed unit can work in conjunction with various cycle configurations using steam turbines, gas turbines, combined cycles with and without cogeneration of thermal loads.

15.6 CONCLUSIONS

The rural energy in India can be better supplied from local power plants, leaving the central power grid to cope with the exclusive requirements of industries and big commercial centres. Biomass is an important source of energy available at the site of power generation which has a huge power potential. The preferred system for burning many types of biomass is fluidised bed combustion with circulating system and bubbling beds more suitable for coarser sized biomass. The fluidised bed units can be used in conjunction with various configurations of power cycles using steam turbines, gas turbines, combined cycles, with and without cogeneration. The ever increasing potential of biomass can be tapped to bring prosperity to rural India.

15.7 REFERENCES

1. M.J. Cook, '*Fluidised Bed Combustion for Burning Biomass*'. International Conference on Fluidised Combustion: Is it achieving its promise? 16/17 October, 1984, London.
2. J.L. Boyen, '*Thermal Energy Recovery*', 2nd Edition, John Wiley and Sons, New York, 1979.
3. S.D. Hu, '*Cogeneration*', Reston Publishing Company Inc., Virginia, 1985.

APPENDICES

Appendix I

LOCAL ENERGY RESOURCES IN VILLAGES

1. Solar energy: 4.5–7.0 kWh/m^2 for 250–300 days/year.
2. Water current energy: Low/Zero head turbines of 200 kW–1000 kW for power generation and lift irrigation. Total potential 5000 MW.
3. Biomass: 200 million tonnes/year plus wood 130 million tonnes/year for 75000 MW power generation by combustion/gasification.
4. Animal wastes: 13.5 kg/day cow dung per cattle to produce 0.46 nm^3 biogas to produce 1 kWh.
5. Wind energy: 100 kWh/m^2–500 kWh/m^2 of turbine swept area to produce 20000 MW for power generation and irrigation water.

Appendix II

RURAL SERVICES REQUIREMENTS

1. Cooking energy: 80 percent of basic rural energy needs, 0.5–1.0 kWh per person per day.
2. Water for irrigarion, drinking and washing:

   25 m^3/hectare-day for drip irrigation of corn, wheat, cotton, millets.

   50–60 m^3/hectare-day for flood irrigation of rice and sugarcane.

   40–50 litres/head-day for livestock.
3. Domestic amenities: Cooking, drinking and wash water, lighting and heating.
4. Community services: Radio and TV sets, street lighting and co-operative milk chilling.
5. Utilities for village industries: Power, water and steam.
6. Food supply system.

Appendix III

ALTERNATE AVAILABLE TECHNOLOGIES

1. Solar cookers: Box type solar cookers, hot plate type solar cookers solar ahara (RECK), biogas plates.
2. Water pumping:

   NPL Abhimanyu solar water pump 1 kW rating using R114, ₹ 37000.

   CEL solar photovoltaic water pumping system 30–40 m^3/day, total head 100 m, ₹ 40000.

   NAL wind mill water pumping system 5 m dia. 23 m^3/day, 20 m depth at wind speed 10 m/s, ₹ 11750.

   Bharat biogas engine 3.7 kW/1500 rpm with 100 × 100 mm centrifugal pump, ₹ 16500.

   Jyoti 5 kW/1500 rpm biogas engine with 100 × 100 mm centrifugal pump, ₹ 37000.

   RECK micro-hydro pumping system as per site conditions.
3. Solar devices, Photovoltaic solar systems for street lighting, TV sets. Solar dryers, kilns, air and water heater, distillation plants. Solar refrigerator, milk cooler, vaccine freezer.
4. Hot water, steam and electricity generation plants: Thermal, solar, photovoltaic, biogas engines, biomass plants, windmills, micro-hydro plants.

Index

F

G

H

I

K

L

M

N

O

P

R

S

T

W

Y

Z